WHAT PEOPLE ARE SAYING ABOU
AND EVERYDAY PRAYERS F

Gina Smith takes readers on a thirty-day journey to
nizes that the most effective pursuit of joy is through ....centered prayer
and praise. Read through this book and feel like one of the many who sit at
Gina's kitchen table, coffee mug in hand, crying out in prayer to the Source
of all joy, Jesus!

—Ronjour and Annie Locke
Instructor, Southeastern Baptist Theological Seminary

Gina reminds us finding joy can be a struggle and Jesus knows that, but
with her insightful words and stories, she gives us the tools to navigate life's
messy, gut-wrenching parts. *Everyday Prayers for Joy* is loaded with deeply
honest and personal revelations, along with biblical truth and practical ways
to live it out. This is one devotional you will come back to again and again.

—Kate Battistelli
Author, *The God Dare*
Co-host, the Mom to Mom Podcast

Open your heart and get ready to receive our friend's wisdom because it's
that of someone who has years of experience not only mothering her own
children and sharing a beautiful love with her husband, but also opening
her doors and heart to countless college students and young couples. Her
constant *yes* to loving others is rare in this world, and it speaks to her heart's
surrender at Jesus' feet. As you read, we pray that this love would flow from
His heart, through her words, right into your spirit and situation.

—Jordan Shimon and Kelsey Shimon
Pastor, NewSong Church, Vienna, VA

Gina Smith is a woman of God's Word. She studies it, seeks it out, and
works hard to apply it in her daily life. She has a heart for prayer and mento-
ring women in their walk with Jesus. That combination means she is worth
listening to!

—Tricia Goyer
Bestselling author, *Praying Through the Bible in a Year*
and *Praying for Your Future Husband*

In the twenty-some years I have known Gina, her walk with God has been a constant example and encouragement. Her humble, compassionate voice teaches us to allow God's Word to shape our souls as we fight for joy on our knees, trusting that as He meets our needs with Himself, He will give us fullness of joy.

—*Stephanie Van Gorden*
Pastor's wife, Hartland Center Community Church, Collins, OH

Gina's heart radiates deep compassion for others exemplified through authenticity as she lives her life to love, teach, encourage others, challenging them to become more like Christ. Her life is a transparent reflection of the spiritually minded friend who has lived this Christian journey in a way that can teach us all.

—*Donna Heindel*
Pastor's wife, Church of the Open Door, York, PA

Gina Smith is the kind of woman you'd meet for coffee and leave with a lifetime friend. She is warm, engaging, wise, full of integrity, and has a wonderful sense of humor. I know you'll be blessed by her words.

—*Susan J. Hein, LPC*
Susan Hein Counseling

While I served overseas as a missionary, Gina's devotions hugged me from across the globe with her tangible, transparent transcriptions of God's Spirit working out His salvation and sanctification in her life. I want to grow ultimately like Christ, but in this life, I'd add, like Gina, from glory to glory until we are before Him with unveiled face.

—*Katie Rymer*
Missionary, International Mission Board

Gina consistently helps me look at the world, and think through the situations I encounter through the lens of the gospel. I listen to her, because I know this commitment of hers to the Word of God is hard-worn. Her guidance comes from her own experience of having to fight for biblical joy when the world presses in. You'll find that kind of attitude, along with a friend who truly desires to serve you, inside *Everyday Prayers for Joy*.

—*Brooke McGlothlin*
Author and cofounder, Million Praying Moms

EVERYDAY PRAYERS

— FOR —

JOY

A 30-Day Devotional & Reflective Journal for Women

GINA L. SMITH

WHITAKER
HOUSE

EVERYDAY PRAYERS FOR JOY
A 30-Day Devotional & Reflective Journal for Women

ginalsmith.com
www.millionprayingmoms.com

ISBN: 978-1-64123-826-7 • eBook ISBN: 978-1-64123-827-4
Printed in the United States of America
© 2022 by Gina L. Smith

Whitaker House
1030 Hunt Valley Circle • New Kensington, PA 15068
www.whitakerhouse.com

Library of Congress Cataloging-in-Publication Data
Names: Smith, Gina L., author.
Title: Everyday prayers for joy : a 30-day devotional & reflective journal
   for women / Gina L. Smith.
Description: New Kensington, PA : Whitaker House, 2022. | Summary: "A
   devotional and reflective journal for women based on the premises that
   the words of the Bible may be used to pray to God, and joy may be found
   during hard times and trying circumstances by focusing on Jesus rather
   than one's blessings"— Provided by publisher.
Identifiers: LCCN 2021045302 (print) | LCCN 2021045303 (ebook) | ISBN
   9781641238267 | ISBN 9781641238274 (ebook)
Subjects: LCSH: Christian women—Religious life—Miscellanea. |
   Joy—Biblical teaching—Miscellanea. |
   Prayer—Christianity—Miscellanea. | Spiritual journals—Authorship. |
   BISAC: RELIGION / Christian Living / Devotional Journal | FAMILY &
   RELATIONSHIPS / Parenting / Motherhood
Classification: LCC BV4527 .S6265 2022 (print) | LCC BV4527 (ebook) | DDC
   248.8/43—dc23
LC record available at https://lccn.loc.gov/2021045302
LC ebook record available at https://lccn.loc.gov/2021045303

1 2 3 4 5 6 7 8 9 10 11 ⨆ 28 27 26 25 24 23 22 21

DEDICATION

To my family: Brian; Brianna and Dani;
Caleb and Nicole.
You have been my support system and cheerleaders,
and have been used by God to help me fight for biblical joy.
You are my greatest sources of joy this side of heaven.

To my mom, Judy Earl.
You have fought for biblical joy your entire life.
Thank you for being a living example of what that looks like!

And to my Savior, the One who gives me a reason
to get up in the morning and promises that there is so much more
to this life than what I can see now. You are my living hope,
the giver of true joy. You enable me to *count it all joy* (James 1:2).
Thank You for allowing me to write about joy. You are so kind.

**Everything if given to God can become
your gateway to joy.**
—*Elisabeth Elliot*

*Count it all joy, my brothers, when you meet trials of various
kinds, for you know that the testing of your faith produces
steadfastness. And let steadfastness have its full effect, that
you may be perfect and complete, lacking in nothing.*
—James 1:2–4

CONTENTS

FOREWORD

Have you ever met someone who just seems to exude joy? An infectious laugh…a beautiful smile…laughter that just draws you in and makes you want to be with them as much as possible? Maybe they have a certain zest for life, a dominating desire to get the most out of every moment, or the ability to find the silver lining of every dark cloud.

I'm not that person.

I've always wanted to be someone who spills over with joy, but my journey to joy has been less natural and more hard-earned. God gifted me with a serious, reserved personality, and I'm a classic overthinker. I love to laugh, and I enjoy a good time as much as anyone else, but my introversion, combined with a tendency to analyze everything to death and feel everything deeply, often makes it hard, if not impossible, for me to let go and let my guard down. I have to choose joy more often than not, not because I have nothing to be thankful for—I do! So much!—but because life can be hard, and I'm the kind of person who takes it personally.

Thankfully, joy doesn't depend on circumstances, and isn't reserved for big, bubbly personalities. It's for everyone—introverts, extroverts, analytical types, happy-go-lucky people, everyone—because joy comes from Jesus.

First Peter 1:8–9 (NIV) says, *"Though you have not seen him, you love him; and even though you do not see him now, you believe in him and are filled with an inexpressible and glorious joy, for you are receiving the end result of your faith, the salvation of your souls."*

I've learned over the years that joy isn't something I can produce or create on my own—at least not true, biblical joy—and that's the kind we all want, right? The kind that lasts, withstands, and even surprises us in the middle of challenging times? According to these verses, joy is something we can be filled with to overflowing just because we know Jesus and are known by Him. But the working out of that truth can be tricky.

Why does Peter tell the people he's talking to that they can be filled with *"inexpressible and glorious joy"* when they can't see God's hand, don't understand why they've been given hardships, and are, perhaps, suffering for their faith? Look at the last part of the verse. It's written right there. They can have glorious joy because they love God, believe in Jesus, and have been given the most important answer to the deepest need of their soul—salvation.

Our salvation is the biggest, truest, fullest reason we can have joy, and that can't be taken away.

In this prayer journal, my dear friend Gina Smith—one of the wisest and most passionately gospel-focused women I know—is going to walk you through her own story of choosing joy, and help you focus on what the Bible says about the subject. She's not taking you on a journey of joy that lasts a few minutes. Her prayer is that as you meditate on, pray through, and become saturated in the truth about biblical joy, God's Word will change your heart to reflect it. In fact, that's kind of the secret of this whole thing. We've both found through our own personal practices that praying God's Word is one of the most powerful forms of prayer there is. Not because it's more holy than other forms, but because God's Word is living and active (Hebrews 4:12) and does exactly what God purposes for it to do (Isaiah 55:11). If that's true, and I wholeheartedly believe it is, prepare yourself to be changed from the inside out as God's Word does what it does best—make you more like Jesus, and fill you with joy that lasts.

Serving together,
Brooke McGlothlin

INTRODUCTION

ON JOY

Joy. It became *my word* a few years ago after God ushered my family and me into a season of very difficult circumstances. It happened one night when I couldn't sleep. I quietly tiptoed out to our living room, sat on the couch, and wrapped myself in a warm blanket. The only light in the room came from three letters that sat on a shelf: "J-O-Y." As I sat there, I reflected on what a difficult season we were in: the loss of a ministry we had been in for over twenty-five years; the loss of both of my husband's parents, who were our biggest support system and cheerleaders; parenting two adult children; and the entrance into the new and mysterious world of anxiety and depression. Little did I know it was only the beginning. We had been thrust into a very long season of unknowns.

That night, I knew that God wanted me to learn His definition of joy. Not merely an intellectual knowledge of the definition—no, that's not what He wanted for me. He wanted joy to be my heart and soul's down-deep experience.

He wanted me to experience joy.

At first, I thought I needed to *choose joy* or *fight for joy* during those difficult days, but it felt like something was missing. As I spent time crying out to God, He made it clear that He wanted me to learn what it means to *"count it all joy."*

Count it all joy, my brothers, when you meet trials of various kinds, for you know that the testing of your faith produces steadfastness. And let steadfastness have its full effect, that you may be perfect and complete, lacking in nothing.

—James 1:2–4

I came to the end of every single resource I had been clinging to and was forced to sit alone before the Lord. He opened my eyes to the fact that often I find joy in the blessings He has provided for me more than I find joy in *Him*, the provider of the blessings. I needed to begin the process of learning what it meant to find joy in Christ alone.

Those difficult days and that life-changing lesson were just the beginning of what God would use to prepare me for the season I am walking through now. We have experienced more losses and life changes since then, and I am learning in an even deeper way how to *"count it all joy"* when my circumstances are hard and life is constantly changing.

Biblical joy is not something that comes and goes; it is not dictated by our circumstances. Biblical joy is something that exists even when we are suffering or going through a heavy trial because it's based on the knowledge that God is present, walking with us in our trials and producing good fruit in us as we go through them. He will use them as a platform to show His work in our lives to those around us.

JOY TRUTHS

1. *God wants Himself and what He is doing in and through our circumstances to be the source of our joy.*

The key to the Christian's joy is our focus in this devotional and reflective journal. Our focus needs to be the God who never changes, is always present, and has promised us an eternity with Him. He is always working His purposes in our life and in the world. We can experience joy in Him, even when we experience sorrow, grief, or pain, because we know He will never forsake us (see Deuteronomy 31:6); He is working all things for our good (see Romans 8:28) and for His glory (see Isaiah 43:7).

2. *We must learn to shift our focus from life circumstances and unknowns, choosing instead to focus on God's purpose.*

God wants to use our suffering as a platform for others to see Him and further the gospel. Nothing can change or steal hard-learned joy in our never-changing, always-present Father. (See Romans 15:13, 1 Thessalonians 5:16–18.) No circumstance can take away the joy we find when we are focusing on God and the grace He has poured out on us and continues to pour out on our lives. (See John 16:14, 22; 2 Corinthians 3:18.) Even in the darkest of times, we can have joy knowing He is working in and through us to show Himself faithful.

3. *Joy is a fruit of the Spirit. We can have real joy even when we are going through very difficult circumstances.*

One of the results of having the Holy Spirit within us is the evidence of His likeness in our everyday lives. Paul calls this *"the fruit of the Spirit"* (Galatians 5:22). It is a testimony to those around us of the reality of God in our lives when the Spirit's joy is present regardless of our circumstances.

God will do what it takes to teach us what it means to find our joy in Him alone, but I must warn you that even after we've experienced what it means, the enemy will continue to fight to make us to find our joy in God's provisions rather than in God Himself. We must learn to discover our joy in God, or life's circumstance will consume us and blind us from seeing His hand in everything. I don't want that, and I know you don't either!

JOY AND THE PRAYER OF LAMENT

When we are in difficult circumstances, we need to be assured that it is okay to ask the hard questions. As long as we're finding the answers to our challenges in God Himself, it's okay. In his book *Trusting God: Even When Life Hurts,* Jerry Bridges described this ongoing process as our "fight with our soul to remember there is a future." He wrote:

Trust is not a passive state of mind. It is a vigorous act of the soul by which we choose to lay hold of the promises of God and cling to them despite the adversity that at times seeks to overwhelm us. Even if the near future looks bleak, there is always an eternal future, so let your gaze break through to eternity.[1]

The prayer of lament is the prayer for a suffering soul. It is our fight with our soul to remember that there is a future. Until recently, I'd never paid much attention to the prayers of lament in the Bible and never thought about using them in my prayer life. Yet after studying them for a while, I've come to believe God gave us the prayers of lament to help us process the suffering we face in this life. When we don't use or understand them, we're actually missing out on the experience of going to the One who loves us most, who can actually heal our hearts and help us to get to the point where our gaze breaks through to eternity. Lamenting is the way we come to God when life is overwhelming.

In the book of Psalms, we see this type of prayer when the writer is facing very difficult circumstances. We see him crying out to God for deliverance from a particular difficulty, often listing his complaints, describing his suffering, and crying out to God for help. In the New Testament, Jesus gave us an example of lamenting when He bore the burden of dying a horrific death on a cross to pay the penalty for the sins of the world. As He went through His agony on the cross, He cried out the words of Psalm 22:1: "*Eli, Eli, lema sabachthani?*' that is, 'My God, my God, why have you forsaken me?*'" (Matthew 27:46; see also Mark 15:34).

LAMENTING: A BIBLICAL MODEL

PRAYERS OF LAMENT ASK QUESTIONS

We often have many questions swimming around in our minds. We ask God why we are experiencing this challenge, why

---

1. Jerry Bridges, *Trusting God: Even When Life Hurts* (Colorado Springs, CO: NavPress, 1988), 214.

He doesn't seem to answer our prayers, where He is in our suffering, how much longer He will allow our suffering to last, and similar queries related to our troubles.

PRAYERS OF LAMENT REMEMBER

We need to come to God with our questions and pour out our hearts to Him, but in a prayer of lament, there is an eventual choice to remember the truth of God's character and His past actions as defined in Scripture. We should not use God's Word as some sort of magic pill that He's prescribing: "Take two verses and call me in the morning." As Bridges pointed out, "We choose to lay hold on the promises of God and cling to them despite the adversity that at times seeks to overwhelm us."[2] This is a choice we will have to make one day at a time, maybe even minute by minute.

PRAYERS OF LAMENT HAVE A GOAL

After we are reminded of who God is and what He has done, God gently and lovingly challenges us to cling to the hope that is found in Him alone.

JOIN ME!

As I wrote each prayer of lament in this book and read each verse, they became the cry of my heart, which then spilled out into the heartfelt prayers that I have shared with you. Writing this book has transformed my way of dealing with life's suffering because it reminded me that not only is it okay to pray this way, it is also a vital tool God has given us to help us process our suffering and allow Him to turn our eyes to Him, finding our joy and hope in who He is, what He has done, and the future He has promised us, His children.

I pray that it will affect you the same way!

We're in this together—crying out and finding our joy and hope in God.

---

2. Ibid.

THE THINK, PRAY, PRAISE
METHOD OF DAILY PRAYER

Brooke McGlothlin
Cofounder, Million Praying Moms

When I first started praying for my own children, I was inspired
by two important truths about God's Word:

1. *The word of God is living and active, sharper than any two-edged sword, piercing to the division of soul and of spirit, of joints and of marrow, and discerning the thoughts and intentions of the heart.* (Hebrews 4:12)

2. God declares, *"My word that goes out from my mouth… will not return to me empty, but will accomplish what I desire and achieve the purpose for which I sent it"* (Isaiah 55:11 NIV)

If those two verses were true—and I believed they were—then it seemed to me that there could be no better thing to pray than God's Word itself! Because this experience was so deeply profound for me, it's the same one I've used to teach other women to pray. I call it my "Think, Pray, Praise" method. It isn't really rocket science, just a practical, biblical way to pray the Word of God over yourself or the people you love. It's also the method we use in Million Praying Moms' Everyday Prayers journal library. Let me walk you through it step by step.

THINK

On each daily page, we give you a verse to pray to make it easy for you to follow this prayer method. However, you can always search the Scriptures for yourself to find a verse you'd like to pray instead. After you've chosen it, reflect on, process, and meditate over your verse. If you have time, read a few verses that come before and after your verse, or even the entire chapter of the Bible so you can have the proper context from which to understand it. Consider what God is speaking to your heart through His Word and through this verse. Dream about the future and what it might look like to see the message of this verse come to fruition in your life, or in your children's lives. In a small way, analyze the verse and figure out what you're inspired to pray.

PRAY

For almost ten years, my desire has been to allow my prayers to be inspired by God's Word. I try very hard not to take verses out of context, or use them for a purpose or meaning other than that which God intended for them. Reading the verse in context, as I just suggested, really helps with this. Once I've selected a verse, I craft it into a prayer. I usually stay as word-for-word as I can and then pray that verse back to God. You can see an example of a "Verse of the Day" and the prayer we craft from it for you on the daily pages of this journal.

Once you have your verse and prayer, use your thoughts about them as a jumping-off point to allow God's Word to move you and shape your prayers.

PRAISE

Praise is my favorite part of this method of prayer! Praising God is like putting on a pair of rose-colored glasses; it literally changes the way you see the world around you.

New York Times bestselling author Ann Voskamp writes:

The brave who focus on all things good and all things beautiful and all things true, even in the small, who give thanks for it and discover joy even in the here and now, they are the change agents who bring the fullest light to all the world. Being joyful isn't what makes you grateful. Being grateful is what makes you joyful.[3]

When we pause to deliberately reflect on the good things God is doing in our lives right now, it changes everything. (This can be even the tiniest of things we have to look hard to see, like having to clean for a Bible study group in your home. You might not want to clean, but at least you have people coming over to discuss the Word of God with you!) Instead of focusing on all we don't have or don't like (such as cleaning), gratitude for what we do have (being with brothers and sisters in Christ) blossoms in our hearts, truly making us joyful. Each day, I try to write down just a few things I'm grateful for, praising God for His continuous work of grace in my life.

BONUS

You might notice the lines for a to-do list on the daily pages. I *love* that little block because I find that when I sit down to pray, my mind gets flooded by all the things I need to do that day. Every. Single. Time. I feel the urgency of my schedule begin to take over, distracting me from the time I so desperately need in God's Word and prayer. Taking a minute to jot down my to-do list before I get started is kind of like doing a *brain dump* each day. If my list is written down, I won't forget what I have to do that day. This frees me up to spend the time I've allocated in prayer without worry stealing it from me.

---

3. Ann Voskamp, *One Thousand Gifts: A Dare to Live Fully Right Where You Are* (Nashville, TN: W Publishing Group, 2010).

PRAYER REQUESTS

Part of being a woman of prayer is interceding on behalf of others. My life literally changed the day a good friend held my hands in hers and said, "Let's pray about this now" instead of telling me, "I'll pray for you." You won't always be able to pray for others in person, but keeping track of their needs on a prayer list like the one at the bottom left of the daily pages is a great way to make sure you're being faithful to cover them in prayer.

GO!

I am so excited about the journey of prayer you hold in your hands. Each day begins with a devotion written specifically for you, and concludes with extra verses and questions for reflection that are a perfect way to take your study of joy to the next level or use with a group. We now consider you part of our Million Praying Moms family! Connect with us at www.millionprayingmoms.com and keep us posted about the things God is doing in your life as you pray.

DAY 1

JOY FOUND IN GOOD GIFTS

READ JAMES 1

Count it all joy, my brothers, when you meet trials of various kinds, for you know that the testing of your faith produces steadfastness. And let steadfastness have its full effect, that you may be perfect and complete, lacking in nothing.

—James 1:2–4

I am facing a trial right now and there is absolutely nothing I can do to change it. These circumstances are completely out of my control and I know that only God can turn things around. Every morning I wake up and I want to take charge and manipulate the situation so it goes the way I want it to, but even if I did try to intervene in some way, there is no guarantee it would improve. In fact, it could actually make things worse!

I have been forced to be quiet and pray. I am having to put my trust in the God who can create something out of nothing, who can turn hearts of stone into hearts of flesh. (See Ezekiel 36:26.) I am being forced to cling to God, one day at a time, and am reminded that any (and all) good that is in my life is because He has allowed it, and when things happen that don't seem so good, I still need to *"count it all joy"* (James 1:2) because they are producing good in me.

James' letter challenges readers to consider what real faith should look like in the life of a believer. He wrote to Christians who were scattered around the world and were experiencing suffering of different kinds, challenging them in a way that, humanly speaking, didn't make sense. He wanted them to learn what it meant to *"count it all joy"* when they experienced trials and reminded them of the work that God could do in their lives when they chose to do that.

How in the world are we supposed to do this? What are we to do when our hearts are broken over fractured family relationships, or we experience the death of a loved one or betrayal in some way? What happens when we lose a job, or experience chronic pain for which our doctor has no explanation? How are we to consider these things as being joyful?

In the first chapter of the book of James, we are told that we should think of our trials as good gifts from God. How can the hard things we face be considered *good* when they often make it difficult to get out of bed each morning? Because we must acknowledge that they are given from the hand of God with the intent of strengthening our faith. If we can choose to see trials this way, the experiences that are normally considered *bad* can actually be the things in which we find joy.

The Christians to whom James originally wrote this letter were experiencing *"trials of many kinds"* (James 1:2 NIV). More than likely, these included poverty and persecution. I don't know about you, but I have never experienced poverty, and any persecution I might have faced over the years has been minimal compared to what these Christians were facing, We all have faced different kinds of trials, and in these verses, James challenges us to view all of our suffering and trials, no matter how big or small, through God's eyes. He wants us to consider them to be sources of joy.

SOMETHING TO THINK ABOUT

James is not telling us we will—or even should—feel happy amidst trials. It's important we understand that the emotions we feel when facing hardship are normal and even God-given. It's okay to cry when we've been hurt, to grieve when we experience loss, and to feel burdened for a child who is struggling. Counting "*it all joy*" means that as we spend time in the presence of God and He helps us see His eternal perspective, we are challenged to cling to God and find our strength in Him. We can "*count it all joy*" because we get to know Him better and experience His grace in time of need. (See Hebrews 4:16.) We get to experience hope when our circumstances seem hopeless. We are given an opportunity to ask for wisdom and hear from Him. We are given an opportunity to witness God's faithfulness. And we are given opportunities to trust Him and watch Him do His work in us and others!

But we must choose this way of thinking. We have to know and speak the truth to ourselves for it to grow in us when we need it most. We may not be in control of our circumstances, but we can control how we view and respond to them.

When you choose to trust God with the things that burden or break your heart, you are choosing to set your mind "*on things that are above, not on things that are on earth*" (Colossians 3:2), to focus on the eternal and not on the temporal (see 2 Corinthians 4:18), and placing your hope in Him and not in the things or people around you (see Psalm 146). When you do this, you can cling to this promise:

> *Blessed is the man who remains steadfast under trial, for when he has stood the test he will receive the crown of life, which God has promised to those who love him.*   —James 1:12

EXTRA VERSES FOR STUDY OR PRAYER

Matthew 5:12; Luke 6:22–23; Romans 5:3; Hebrews 11:36; 1 Peter 1:6–8.

VERSES OF THE DAY

Count it all joy, my brothers, when you meet trials of various kinds, for you know that the testing of your faith produces steadfastness. And let steadfastness have its full effect, that you may be perfect and complete, lacking in nothing.

—James 1:2–4

PRAYER

Father, this is a hard command to follow! You say You will enable me to control how I respond in difficult circumstances even though I'm not in control of them. Help me today to remember Your promise that the testing of my faith produces steadfastness, and there is a purpose in all of my suffering. Help me learn, grow stronger, and rejoice as it happens!

THINK:

_____

_____

_____

PRAY:

_____

_____

_____

PRAISE:

_____

_____

_____

TO DO: PRAYER LIST:

_____   _____

_____   _____

_____   _____

QUESTIONS FOR DEEPER REFLECTION

1. When has God used a time of trial to do something in and through you? What was it that helped you persevere in that trial?

   _____

   _____

2. In your own words, describe what it means to *"count it all joy"* during a trial?

   _____

   _____

   _____

DAY 2

JOY FOUND IN
OUR LIVING HOPE

READ 1 PETER 1

Though you have not seen him, you love him. Though you do not now see him, you believe in him and rejoice with joy that is inexpressible and filled with glory, obtaining the outcome of your faith, the salvation of your souls.   —1 Peter 1:8–9

We hadn't had a vacation in some time and decided that it would be a good idea to go to the beach. I hoped to find a spot we hadn't visited before and wanted to find a house that was roomy enough to allow our children and their spouses to join us.

I eagerly visited rental websites and carefully studied picture after picture of beautiful beach homes. After reading descriptions, reviews, and ratings of several homes, I finally found something that seemed perfect for our needs and desires, so I reserved what I pictured to be a beautiful home in a picturesque setting.

For the next few weeks, we dreamed of a perfect beach vacation—the meals we'd make, the games we'd play, laying on the beach, taking walks, and enjoying each other as a family. The excitement and anticipation of what was ahead carried me through the days leading up to our departure.

When the day finally arrived, we packed our car and excitedly traveled to our destination. When we got there, the reality was drastically different from the picture we had in our minds and what was on the website.

The recently renovated beach house was located in an unsafe area. The beach and the boardwalk were abandoned. The photos that had been posted online were of improvements that had been made in an attempt to attract potential vacationers to the once crowded and thriving beach community. Additionally, there was little to do where we were staying, causing us to drive some distance to find decent food or activities.

Although we had an enjoyable time together as a family, the location and the few days we spent there were ultimately disappointing. What we had anticipated for weeks ended up being nothing like what had been promised. We had set our hopes on a beautiful location and it let us down.

The book of 1 Peter describes how blessed we are in Christ, and it talks about our *"living hope"* that exists because of the death and resurrection of Jesus. (See 1 Peter 1:3.) Peter describes the inheritance we have as God's children, a promised inheritance that gives us purpose and a reason to have joy amidst suffering. Because of that promise, we have reason to have joy as we wait for, and anticipate, what we know awaits us.

First Peter 1:8–9 tells us that even though we have not laid eyes on God, we can love Him. Because He first loved us, not only can we learn to love Him, but His love for us prompts Him to reveal Himself in such a mysterious way that we can experience Him, know Him, and love Him even when we haven't physically seen Him. Because He opens our eyes to the truths in His Word, we can have relationship with Him. This truth enables us to persevere even though we are strangers and aliens in this world. Even though we experience suffering on this earth, we can persevere with joy in our hearts, knowing we will not be disappointed in heaven, and we can be confident that God will bring to pass what He has promised. This living hope gives purpose to our life and trials. This knowledge should provoke a deeper love and dependence in our hearts for Him.

SOMETHING TO THINK ABOUT

Joy is not something we will only experience in the future when all things are made new, when we receive the promised inheritance, or when we see Jesus face to face. Joy is something we can experience today, one day at a time, as we choose to cling to Him, His promises, and the hope that comes from looking to the ultimate joy that will come on that final day.

We will not be disappointed!

EXTRA VERSES FOR STUDY OR PRAYER

Isaiah 35:10; John 20:29; 2 Corinthians 4:18; Ephesians 3:19.

VERSES OF THE DAY

Though you have not seen him, you love him. Though you do not now see him, you believe in him and rejoice with joy that is inexpressible and filled with glory, obtaining the outcome of your faith, the salvation of your souls.   —1 Peter 1:8–9

PRAYER

Father, thank You for the gift of Your Son. I can't see Him, but I love Him because He first loved me. Today, may the joy of my salvation overflow through everything I do and say so those around me will be drawn to Him.

THINK:

_____

_____

_____

PRAY:

_____

_____

_____

PRAISE:

_____

_____

_____

TO DO: PRAYER LIST:

_____   _____

_____   _____

_____   _____

QUESTIONS FOR DEEPER REFLECTION

1. Is it difficult at times for you to feel like you really love God when you can't physically see Him? If so, what do you do during those times?

_____

_____

2. What verses can you think of that help you push past times of doubt and understand what it means to love someone you can't see?

_____

_____

DAY 3

JOY FOUND IN
THE GOD OF HOPE

READ ROMANS 15

May the God of hope fill you with all joy and peace in believing, so that by the power of the Holy Spirit you may abound in hope. —Romans 15:13

For as long as I can remember, I desired to go to a Christian college to prepare for some kind of full-time career in ministry. I also desired to go to a school where I would be surrounded by a Christian community of believers my age, and, of course, my hope was that I might meet and marry a man who was committed to Jesus and had been called to being in full-time ministry as well.

During my senior year of high school, it became evident that I would not be able to afford to pay for college and my dream of going to a Christian college would not be coming true. I would need to live at home, find a job, and work full-time. After graduating from high school, I spent the summer traveling with a mission team. It was an amazing experience that caused the growth of that long-time desire to attend a Christian college, study the Bible, and prepare for some kind of career in ministry. But at the end of that summer, I returned home and was faced with the reality that most of my friends had left for college and I had been left behind with unfulfilled dreams. I was heartbroken.

I found a job working at a retail store at the local mall. I was miserable. Each day, I would get up, get dressed, and drive to a job I hated. With each passing day, I began to lose hope that what I longed to do with my life would ever materialize. Finally, having lost hope, I concluded that God had forgotten me, and I attempted to end my life.

There have been very few times in my life since then that I have been so blinded to any evident hope. As I have gotten older, I have learned where my hope and purpose lie, even in the hardest of times. But at the age of eighteen, I did not fully comprehend that reality. I did not know how to look to the God of hope to find joy and peace in what seemed like impossible circumstances.

God was so merciful to me, carrying me through those hopeless and dark days. I will forever be grateful for the precious people He brought into my life to help strengthen me in God and who came alongside me as I grew in my faith. Four years after graduating from high school, my dream finally came true. After working full-time and praying for God to provide the money I needed, I found myself on a Christian college campus. I was beyond excited to be there and it didn't take long before I was soaking up every aspect of the experience I could—Christian community, close friends, dorm life, independence, godly mentors, laughter, all-nighters, late-night runs for junk food, weekend trips home with friends, and, of course, the opportunity to be immersed in the study of God's Word. I was living my dream!

Romans is a book that tells us how Jesus became the hope not only of the Jews but also the Gentiles. Our verse for today is a prayer Paul prayed for God's people. His desire was that they might experience hope, joy, peace, and power.

God is a God of hope. In fact, one of His most beautiful names is *the God of hope*. He alone is the one source of hope we have in this life, and He is the One who gives life meaning. In my young, eighteen-year-old mind, I thought my joy and peace depended on the fulfillment of my dreams and desires. I didn't know what God had planned for my future and it felt like He had forgotten me. Of course, now I know that He never does.

SOMETHING TO THINK ABOUT

Paul's desire was that believers trust in God and, in so doing, experience a growing faith that would cause true joy to well up inside their hearts, giving stability no matter the circumstances. He knew this would help them persevere in their walk with God and turn any unbelief into solid, unwavering confidence in God. Paul fervently prayed, asking God to give more than just hope based on the promises of changing circumstances or getting what they desired. No, he wanted more for them, praying that they would experience a hope that only the Holy Spirit could produce, given only by the promise of our Father and God of hope!

In the same way that Paul experienced this for himself and prayed this for his fellow believers, we can experience this firsthand and turn our experience into a prayer for our fellow brothers and sisters in Christ. Are you filled with joy and peace? Are you abounding in hope? This is God's desire for the heart and mind of every believer.

Note: If you are considering taking your own life, please reach out to a pastor, friend, or suicide hotline. From my experience, I can tell you that you have better options—and I'm praying for you!

EXTRA VERSES FOR STUDY OR PRAYER

Psalm 96:12; Isaiah 55:12; John 14:1–27; Romans 14:17.

VERSE OF THE DAY

May the God of hope fill you with all joy and peace in believing, so that by the power of the Holy Spirit you may abound in hope.   —Romans 15:13

PRAYER

Father, You are the only lasting source of hope I have for meaning in this life and my hope for eternal life. Help me trust in You today, and please grow my faith, for I know it's the only way I will experience true joy and peace.

THINK:

_____

_____

_____

PRAY:

_____

_____

PRAISE:

_____

_____

_____

TO DO: PRAYER LIST:

_____   _____

_____   _____

_____   _____

QUESTIONS FOR DEEPER REFLECTION

1. Have you experienced a time when it seemed like you had no hope? What were the circumstances that caused you to feel that way?

_____

_____

_____

2. What Scripture verses can you think of that might give you hope when you find yourself feeling hopeless?

_____

_____

_____

DAY 4

JOY FOUND IN BEING FOUND

READ LUKE 15

Just so, I tell you, there will be more joy in heaven over one sinner who repents than over ninety-nine righteous persons who need no repentance. —Luke 15:7

My husband's father was one of the kindest, most generous, and godly men I've ever known. He grew up in the 1930s and '40s, when many of the citizens of our country embraced what would be considered more conservative values. In fact, the majority of the people in our country would probably have considered themselves to be Christian and attended church regularly. My father-in-law went home to be with Jesus in 2016, right before his ninetieth birthday, but I can still remember how he would talk about the way things used to be, how the world had changed so drastically from when he was growing up, and how he was seeing things happen that he never imagined he would see in his lifetime.

A few months before my father-in-law passed, my husband and I traveled the familiar road to the retirement community where he had been living for twelve years. He needed round-the-clock nursing care and was connected to a monitor that constantly kept track of his vital signs. That day, when we walked into his little one-room apartment, he was watching the news on TV. We joined him on the couch and began talking about the events being reported.

After a few minutes, a nurse walked into the room to check his vital signs. "Mr. Smith," she said, "I think you should turn off the news. Your heart rate is up because you are stressed."

He adamantly assured her that he felt fine, but the monitor revealed another story. He was unaware of the way his body was responding to the disturbing events he was seeing played out on the news. The nurse turned the television off and suggested that we keep it off for the rest of the day.

We are living in a world that has quickly become increasingly evil. How are you affected by what you see being lived out in our society and in the world? As Bible-believing Christians, we are definitely in the minority. Like my father-in-law, I see things going on in our world that I never thought I'd see in my lifetime, and I easily find myself stressed and tempted toward the faulty thinking that our world is in a hopeless state. But when I read the parables found in Luke 15, I am reminded that this way of thinking is far from biblical and not an accurate reflection of the heart of God.

Each parable in Luke 15 talks about something valuable that was lost and how it was found. Jesus shared these parables because the Pharisees were bothered that He was being invited into the homes of those they considered to be sinners. Although they didn't mind Jesus and His teachings, they did not like that He spent time with those who were considered outcasts or undesirables. Jesus answered the Pharisees by telling them about a lost sheep, a lost coin, and a lost son. As He told each parable, He shared how God views those who are lost and the lengths to which He will go to find them and bring them to safety.

In the parable of the lost sheep, we see the Lord leaving the ninety-nine sheep that are not lost and going to search for the one that has wandered away. When He finally finds this one lost sheep, He picks it up, lays it on His shoulders, and carries it home to safety. After He arrives home, He gathers everyone around Him and throws a party, celebrating that this one that was lost has been found. Our verse of the day represents the heart of a loving Shepherd who has found His lost sheep.

SOMETHING TO THINK ABOUT

The picture of the celebration over one lost sheep that's been found and rescued is the essence of God's heart: each person who is lost has value and is made in His image. There are no outcasts in His eyes. All of the lost are loved ones to be pursued, found, and saved. In these verses, we see the joy that God and all the hosts of heaven feel when a lost one is found. No matter how bad things get in this world, it is not beyond hope because God is still in the business of seeking out those who are lost.

We can face each day with hope because we know God is a God who still seeks and saves the lost. If we have been found and saved, we can have joy in our hearts, regardless of our circumstances, because we know we are saved and kept for all eternity by a loving Father who found us, placed us on His shoulders, carried us home, and gave us new life in Him. We can have everlasting joy knowing all of heaven joined with God and threw a party when we were rescued.

That's how precious we all are to God.

EXTRA VERSES FOR STUDY OR PRAYER

Matthew 18:13; Luke 15:6, 10, 32.

VERSE OF THE DAY

Just so, I tell you, there will be more joy in heaven over one sinner who repents than over ninety-nine righteous persons who need no repentance. —Luke 15:7

PRAYER

Father, thank You for opening my eyes to the gospel and showing me my desperate need for a Savior. There is no greater miracle than that of a person whose heart is changed. I know You are the only one who can make that change in me. Thank You for rejoicing over me!

THINK:

_____

_____

_____

PRAY:

_____

_____

_____

PRAISE:

_____

_____

_____

TO DO: PRAYER LIST:

_____   _____

_____   _____

_____   _____

QUESTIONS FOR DEEPER REFLECTION

1. Is it hard for you to understand the love God has for you? Why do you think there is so much joy in heaven when one sinner repents?

_____

_____

_____

2. Can you think of a specific time when you realized you needed to repent and turned your life over to God? If so, record that date or the period of time when it became clear to you.

_____

_____

_____

DAY 5

THE JOY OF
THE LORD IS MY STRENGTH

READ NEHEMIAH 8

Then he said to them, "Go your way. Eat the fat and drink sweet wine and send portions to anyone who has nothing ready, for this day is holy to our Lord. And do not be grieved, for the joy of the LORD is your strength." —Nehemiah 8:10

As my children entered into the years when they were more aware of their failures and began learning what it meant to have a genuine sorrow for something they had done wrong, I felt an urgency to walk them from their sorrow and repentance to encouragement for the growth that was happening in their lives. I wanted them to know, without a shadow of a doubt, that they were forgiven and loved unconditionally, but I also wanted them to see the bigger picture. Even if they made a poor choice or messed up in some way, I wanted them to see they were in a process of growth, learning, and maturity. When they would say, "I'm sorry I failed, Mom," I would say, "You are learning. That's a good thing!" I wanted them to move beyond sorrow and into the encouragement of seeing their own growth.

Now that my children are grown and married, we are able to encourage each other with this truth. As we have been learning over the past three-and-a-half years to navigate being the parents of married children, we have not done things perfectly. In fact, we have actually messed up quite a few times. As my children have been learning to prioritize their spouses and live their own lives, there have been some hurt feelings. We've been figuring out how we all fit into each other's lives, and it is a hard transition! We have had to remind each other on several occasions that we are learning. We try not to focus on the failure, but on asking for forgiveness and on learning how to move forward in a better way.

In the book of Nehemiah, we see that Nehemiah had been appointed to be governor, and although he had a lot of pushback and resistance, he did not waver in his quest to rebuild the temple. He relied on the strength and provision of God and got the job done. Nehemiah wanted the people to be filled with gratefulness to God for how He had provided for them and protected them, but they were not thankful and they were not rejoicing.

After reading the Word of God (the Law), they realized they had not been following His ways. The people wept because they realized they had not lived in a way that glorified God. Initially, weeping was the appropriate response. It showed they had soft, repentant hearts. But they couldn't stay there weeping. They had to move beyond it. Because God is a loving Father, He wanted them to be restored and brought into a place of growth and learning. He wanted them to experience joy!

In verse 10, Nehemiah told the Israelites they did not need to be sad. He knew they were repentant and wanted to follow the ways of God. That alone was something to rejoice over! But he wanted them to also see that they were invited to leave their past behind them and move into a new way of living. They could rejoice in their new devotion to God. They didn't need to walk in condemnation because of their failure.

Nehemiah told his people, *"Do not be grieved, for the joy of the Lord is your strength."* What did he mean by that?

When our eyes are opened to the fact that we are not condemned even though we have failed, and we are not defined by our failure, we can move beyond our tears of repentance and into a state of rejoicing in the Lord. We find strength when we focus on truth and our weeping can turn into the joy of the Lord!

We are strongest when we choose the joy of the Lord.

We find strength to persevere when we choose the joy of the Lord.

We are able to resist attack when we choose the joy of the Lord.

SOMETHING TO THINK ABOUT

The joy of the Lord is not an emotion. We experience it when we choose to move beyond our failures and focus on the grace God has poured out on us, the forgiveness He offers us, and the truths of His Word that keep us learning and growing. The joy of the Lord is meant to be what gives us our spiritual energy, muscle, and power. It is our sustaining strength.

Yes, we might weep when we repent from the sin God exposes in our lives. But when we understand and cling to the Word of God, we can move forward into rejoicing as His precious promises become a reality in our lives, in the same way that the Israelites found hope and learned that the joy of the Lord was their strength.

EXTRA VERSES FOR STUDY OR PRAYER

Deuteronomy 26:11–13; Psalm 28:7–8; Ecclesiastes 2:24; 3:13.

VERSE OF THE DAY

Then he said to them, "Go your way. Eat the fat and drink sweet wine and send portions to anyone who has nothing

ready, for this day is holy to our Lord. And do not be grieved,
for the joy of the LORD *is your strength."* —Nehemiah 8:10

PRAYER

Father, I know that the more time I spend in Your Word, gaining a better understanding of it, the more comfort I will find in what is written there. Help me to get to know You better so that I might find the strength and joy You provide to those who belong to You. I pray You would renew my spiritual strength so that, as You promise in Isaiah 40:31, I can *"run and not be weary"* and *"walk and not faint."*

THINK:

_____

_____

_____

PRAY:

_____

_____

_____

PRAISE:

_____

_____

_____

TO DO: PRAYER LIST:

_____   _____

_____   _____

_____   _____

QUESTIONS FOR DEEPER REFLECTION

1. Do you have difficulty finding time to be in the Word? What are the things that get in the way of you doing this?

_____

_____

_____

2. What will you do this week to make time to do what is most important?

_____

_____

_____

DAY 6

JOY FOUND
IN REFRESHING OTHERS

READ PHILEMON 1

For I have derived much joy and comfort from your love, my brother, because the hearts of the saints have been refreshed through you. —Philemon 1:7

I will never forget the days I spent with my friend Bonnie. She welcomed me into her home and family in a way that I'd never experienced before. She spent time with me even though I was a rough-around-the-edges, immature college student, and she lovingly encouraged me through the years of early motherhood. Her home was filled with love, encouragement, laughter, simple hospitality, and, most importantly, a humble, servant-hearted love for Jesus. She taught me how to love my husband and children, and she taught me about God through her example and our times of Bible study. I will always be grateful for those years we spent together.

Bonnie's home had been transformed by the gospel and she was a true giver of much grace. I never heard a negative word out of her mouth, and during the few times that I witnessed her face some hurtful situations with fellow believers, she always spoke about them in a positive light. I knew that she was always ready to forgive and would be one to show grace. I am confident that even to this day, she would fully embrace and love any person regardless of who they are or what they had done.

Her life and example have stayed with me over the years even though we lost touch. She is someone I have sought to emulate over the years and immediately comes to mind when I read today's verse.

Paul had spent three years in Ephesus, preaching the gospel. During that time, a very wealthy man named Philemon heard the gospel, was saved, and immediately began opening his home for believers to meet. He wanted to serve God in any way possible.

Onesimus, one of Philemon's servants, stole something from his master's home and fled to Rome, hoping to blend into this highly populated city and not be found. In God's sovereignty, Onesimus came into contact with Paul, heard the gospel, gave his life to Christ, and became a friend and helper to Paul, who was imprisoned in Rome. Paul, knowing that Onesimus was a fugitive and had broken relationships that needed to be taken care of, wrote to Philemon, telling him how Onesimus's life had been transformed. Paul appealed to him to welcome Onesimus back into his home "*as a beloved brother*" (verse 16). He encouraged Philemon to have a new relationship with his former servant, something that would have been very difficult and rare in the Greco-Roman culture of the day. Paul wanted to see radical reconciliation.

SOMETHING TO THINK ABOUT

How did Paul know that he could make this appeal to Philemon? He had been in his home. He had seen, firsthand, his transformed life after hearing and receiving the gospel, and how Philemon had deeply loved and served the believers there.

As Paul says in verse 7, "*The hearts of the saints have been refreshed through you.*" Philemon had a reputation for loving his brothers and sisters in Christ and being a great encouragement to them. Just the memory of his time with Philemon brought Paul great joy. Remembering the love he had experienced in his home gave Paul the confidence to appeal to Philemon to receive his former slave back into his home, view him through eyes of grace, and love him as the brother in Christ he had become.

Do you know someone who, after spending time together, leaves you feeling refreshed and encouraged? More importantly, do you bring joy to others by seeking to refresh them? Are you known to be approachable and willing to forgive and love those who have hurt you? I love that Paul knew he could appeal to Philemon because of his friendship. He knew he could send the offender back to the offended and they would become beloved brothers.

EXTRA VERSES FOR STUDY OR PRAYER

Second Corinthians 7:4, 13; 1 Thessalonians 3:9; Philemon 1:20.

VERSE OF THE DAY

For I have derived much joy and comfort from your love, my brother, because the hearts of the saints have been refreshed through you.   —Philemon 1:7

PRAYER

Father, I pray that You would give me a heart for others and that I would grow in my love for those whom You have put in my life. Please show me today who You want me to reach out to, to encourage and refresh. Please help me to be willing to give generously from all that You have blessed me with, that others might experience the joy and comfort that comes from You.

THINK:

PRAY:

_____

_____

_____

PRAISE:

_____

_____

_____

TO DO: PRAYER LIST:

QUESTIONS FOR DEEPER REFLECTION

1. Can you think of a time when you were refreshed after spending time with someone? What was it about that person that caused you to feel refreshed?

_____

_____

2. Can you think of a person or persons you could refresh today? If so, how will you do that?

_____

_____

DAY 7

JOY FOUND IN WORSHIP

READ PSALM 27

And now my head shall be lifted up above my enemies all around me, and I will offer in his tent sacrifices with shouts of joy; I will sing and make melody to the LORD. —Psalm 27:6

We see two sides of David in this particular psalm: a confident David and a desperate David. He is confident that God is able to protect him...and desperate for God to rescue him from his enemies. He's confident because he has experienced God's goodness in the past...and desperate for God's assurance that He will come to his aid in the future.

David trusts confidently in the Lord. He knows that God is able to protect him. He has seen it happen over and over again. But David also pleads with God for deliverance from those who are seeking his life in the present. He knows what God is capable of, but he still is fearful of those who seek his life.

Can you relate to David as he moves from confidence to fear? I sure can! Even though it may not make sense, we can be confident in God and His promises and yet still experience anxiety or fear. That is a normal human response.

So what does David do? He makes a choice. He joyfully offers sacrifices to the Lord and sings to Him. He begins to thank God. He remembers the promises that he has been given.

Remembering the promise of God's presence caused David to rejoice and offer thanks; it gave him something to hold on to when facing fearful circumstances. He followed these memories with worship because He remembered all that God had done and the victories He had won. This filled him with gratitude and joy.

SOMETHING TO THINK ABOUT

When we seek God, we are promised that we will receive God's strength. *"The eyes of the LORD range throughout the earth to strengthen those whose hearts are fully committed to him"* (2 Chronicles 16:9 NIV). We are not immune from all trouble, but we can have a sense of safety and the knowledge that God is faithful in the midst of our troubles. We can have this same confidence in all of life's circumstances.

I love David's example of offering a sacrifice of joy. He chose to focus on the victories and provisions of God when he was in the midst of fear and danger. That meant he had to rise above any dread and anxiety he was feeling and choose to focus on that which would give him hope.

When we choose to worship God, we are taking advantage of our privilege of having unhindered access to God and His presence; we are choosing to dwell in safety and joy regardless of what is going on around us. We are choosing to offer a sacrifice of joy.

EXTRA VERSES FOR STUDY OR PRAYER

Psalm 3:3; Psalm 13:6; Psalm 95:1; Psalm 107:22.

VERSE OF THE DAY

And now my head shall be lifted up above my enemies all around me, and I will offer in his tent sacrifices with shouts of joy; I will sing and make melody to the LORD. —Psalm 27:6

PRAYER

Father, I praise and thank You for all You have done in my life. You have been so merciful to me. You are the Father of mercies, the God of all comfort, and the One who gives all blessings. Help me be aware of You today and to be thankful for all You have done in my life. I will offer sacrifices of praise to You today with a joyful heart.

THINK:

PRAY:

PRAISE:

TO DO: PRAYER LIST:

QUESTIONS FOR DEEPER REFLECTION

1. Take some time to look back over your life. Can you see how God has been merciful to you?

2. What can you do today to become more aware of God's mercy in your day-to-day life?

DAY 8

JOY FOUND
IN AN APT ANSWER

READ PROVERBS 15

*To make an apt answer is a joy to a man, and a word in
season, how good it is!* —Proverbs 15:23

We were leaving church one Sunday after the morning service
when we were stopped by Phil, a dear friend, who asked us how
we were doing. I find great encouragement in speaking with Phil
because I know that whenever we talk, it's because he is sincerely
interested in what we have to say. He will always share honestly
what he has been going through and how God is teaching him. I
think I have left every conversation with him feeling blessed.

On this particular Sunday, he shared with us what God had
been teaching him as he had gone through significant changes in
his life and work. He shared honestly how he felt at the beginning
of the trial and how God used His Word in these circumstances to
give him a big-picture, biblical perspective. Having gone through
a similar change in our own lives, my husband and I listened carefully as Phil spoke. This short conversation on the way to our car
on a Sunday morning ended up being one of those life-changing,
perspective-adjusting, inspiring conversations that are needed and
experienced at just the right time.

As we were saying goodbye, I told Phil that I appreciated his
sharing what he did and that I had really needed to hear the lessons

he had been learning. He humbly responded by saying, "Was that helpful? Good! I'm so glad to hear that!"

An apt answer and a *good word* can refer to any number of conversation pieces: instruction, counsel, or advice given, an appropriate answer, or an exhortation. Any word that is spoken at just the right time can be used by God to direct or encourage another person. These words have the potential and the power to impact another for good and to serve as a ministry of the Holy Spirit through that person who is tuned in to Him and open to His leading as he asks God to use him and his words. It is a service to others when our speech is *"gracious, seasoned with salt"* (Colossians 4:6). It is a ministry of grace to the one listening.

These words can also bring joy to the one speaking them. What a grace we have been given to be used by God to speak His words to others. What a blessing it is to know that we have somehow opened our mouths and given words of refreshment to strengthen a brother or sister in Christ.

SOMETHING TO THINK ABOUT

We speak many words in one day. Our words have the power to build up and bless, or tear down and discourage. The more we are filled up with God's Word and are open to the leading of His Spirit, the more likely it will be that we will be used by Him to speak *"an apt answer"* and *"a word in season."* Interestingly enough, not only does God use our words in the lives of others, but being used by God in another person's life will bring joy to our lives as well.

God's ways really are best, aren't they?

EXTRA VERSES FOR STUDY OR PRAYER
Proverbs 12:14; 16:13; 25:11; Isaiah 50:4.

VERSE OF THE DAY

To make an apt answer is a joy to a man, and a word in season, how good it is! —Proverbs 15:23

PRAYER

Father, I pray that the words that I speak today will be words that bring joy to others. I pray that my heart would be tuned in to Your Spirit so that I can answer others with the words You want me to use, and that it will be a blessing to them.

THINK:

_____

_____

_____

PRAY:

_____

_____

_____

PRAISE:

_____

_____

_____

TO DO: PRAYER LIST:

_____   _____

_____   _____

_____   _____

QUESTIONS FOR DEEPER REFLECTION

1. What kind of things do other people do that bless you or bring you joy?

_____

_____

_____

2. Can you think of someone who has spoken *"an apt answer"* to you at just the right time? Maybe you can do the same for them by contacting them and telling them how they have been an encouragement to you and how God used them in your life.

_____

_____

_____

DAY 9

JOY FOUND IN THE MORNING

READ PSALM 30

Sing praises to the Lord, *O you his saints, and give thanks to his holy name. For his anger is but for a moment, and his favor is for a lifetime. Weeping may tarry for the night, but joy comes with the morning….You have turned for me my mourning into dancing; you have loosed my sackcloth and clothed me with gladness, that my glory may sing your praise and not be silent. O* Lord *my God, I will give thanks to you forever!*
—Psalm 30:4–5, 11–12

It's like a breath of fresh air, a warm spring morning after a long cold winter, the opening of a window, or the smell of blooming flowers wafting into a sunlit kitchen. It's like an icy cold drink of lemonade on a hot summer day, or waking up fully refreshed after a good night's sleep. What am I talking about? The joy that comes in the morning!

But what exactly does that mean? This has been one of my favorite passages of Scripture to study because it describes so beautifully how I have felt a number of times in my life!

In Psalm 30, we see that David has just come out of a time where he has experienced God delivering him from the attacks of his enemies, answering prayer when he was desperate, healing him when he was sick, and rescuing him from death. His time of weeping has come to an end. He is now in a time of peace and refreshment. He is experiencing the joy that comes in the morning.

God has given him some relief from his suffering!

Pictured in this psalm is a man whose heart is full to overflowing with thanksgiving. David reflects on his life, which has been saturated with God's care, deliverance, and provision. Overwhelmed, David shares his experience so that anyone who hears can learn to view their own lives in the same way. He proclaims his desire to *"extol the* LORD *at all times"* (Psalm 34:1 NIV), to sing praises and give thanks, and he encourages those with him to do the same.

SOMETHING TO THINK ABOUT

We have all been through times of weeping. Whether this time has lasted for months or years, weeks or days, there is joy when we are brought out into a season of relief and rest. But this season of joy is not meant solely for our own personal refreshment. Like David, we can take the time to reflect on our times of weeping and see all the ways God has strengthened, sustained, and helped us. We can proclaim His goodness when we share all of the big and small evidence of His hand in our lives as He guides us and helps us to persevere. When we see all that He has done, we can do what David did in these verses—extol and enthusiastically praise our God!

EXTRA VERSES FOR STUDY OR PRAYER

Psalm 16:11; Psalm 21:6; Psalm 36:7–9; Psalm 63:3; Psalm 126:5.

VERSE OF THE DAY

For his anger is but for a moment, and his favor is for a lifetime. Weeping may tarry for the night, but joy comes with the morning. —Psalm 30:5

PRAYER

Father, thank You for Your promise that the suffering and weariness that I experience are temporary. The pain, grief, sorrow, and sickness I am going through will not have the final word in my life. *You* will have the final word. Joy *will* come in the morning. Thank You for Your promise that joy will come and that one day, all of our tears will be wiped away from our eyes for all eternity.

THINK:

_____

_____

_____

PRAY:

_____

_____

_____

PRAISE:

_____

_____

_____

TO DO: PRAYER LIST:

_____   _____

_____   _____

_____   _____

QUESTIONS FOR DEEPER REFLECTION

1. Are you feeling weary today? If so, what has brought you to this point?

2. Read today's verse again. What does it say and how does it encourage you?

DAY 10

JOY FOUND
IN LOVING OUR BROTHER

READ ROMANS 14

*For the kingdom of God is not a matter of eating and drinking
but of righteousness and peace and joy in the Holy Spirit.*
—Romans 14:17

In my very early days of motherhood, I went through a season when I saw everything as either black or white, right or wrong, good or bad. With a fearful heart, and in an effort to attempt to take control of everything that might affect my home and children, I started down the dangerous and toxic road of legalism. The issues that may have started as convictions in my life quickly became *the law*. Sadly, while in this way of thinking, what I considered to be discernment as I processed certain issues actually resulted in the judgment of those who did things differently than me.

Thankfully, God opened my eyes to the destructive road I was on and He gently led me into a more biblical way of viewing life and others. To this day, I have a hard time looking at photos that were taken during those early days. While others might see a younger version of myself and my family, what I see is the heart attitude that characterized me back then. It grieves me when I think of what I imposed on my children and others.

In Romans 14, we see Paul bravely addressing how believers are called to treat each other when they have different convictions about issues when there are no clear answers. He addresses those believers who felt free to do things that were formerly forbidden under the law of Moses. He basically tells them, "Don't flaunt your freedom! Don't judge each other! Don't hold onto your freedom if it causes someone else to stumble." He was encouraging believers to accept each other even when they differ on some convictions. Paul may have sided with a particular group, but he encouraged them all to not despise those who thought differently.

The faith of another believer is more important than our opinions on less important issues. We need to always relate to each other in love, even if we don't agree on some things.

SOMETHING TO THINK ABOUT

It is easy to move into an unloving and judgmental way of thinking. It takes a lot of prayer, time in the Word, and nurturing our relationship with God for this sinful attitude of the heart to be exposed and changed. Sometimes it can be so subtle that we don't even recognize it for what it is.

It is important to remember that although our freedom in Christ and our convictions are important, they are not the main point. The ultimate prize is the kingdom of God. We are righteous because God says we are righteous as soon as we accept His free gift of salvation. Peace and joy come because we are given the Holy Spirit. Our security does not come from our actions but from our relationship with God.

We are never justified in having a critical or judgmental attitude toward another individual, or in proudly declaring our *freedom in Christ*. Our focus should be on strengthening our brothers and sisters in Christ, loving them, and thanking God for His blessings as members of the body of Christ.

EXTRA VERSES FOR STUDY OR PRAYER

Matthew 6:33; 7:16; Romans 15:13; Galatians 5:22.

VERSE OF THE DAY

For the kingdom of God is not a matter of eating and drinking but of righteousness and peace and joy in the Holy Spirit.
—Romans 14:17

PRAYER

Father, thank You for declaring me righteous in Your eyes, and thank You that my place with You is secure. I know I can depend on Christ's death on the cross that has covered my sin, and I don't have to do anything to earn my salvation. Help me to experience the peace and joy that only your Spirit can give as I walk in this reality today.

THINK:

_____

_____

_____

PRAY

_____

_____

_____

PRAISE:

_____

_____

_____

TO DO: PRAYER LIST:

_____   _____

_____   _____

_____   _____

QUESTIONS FOR DEEPER REFLECTION

1. What does it mean to be declared righteous in God's eyes?

_____

_____

_____

2. How does that happen? Does this truth encourage you and give you peace and joy?

_____

_____

_____

DAY 11

JOY FOUND IN BEING READY

READ 1 THESSALONIANS 5

Rejoice always, pray without ceasing, give thanks in all circumstances; for this is the will of God in Christ Jesus for you.
—1 Thessalonians 5:16–18

When we read this verse all by itself, it might seem like an awful lot to ask of a believer. How are we supposed to actually pray without ceasing and give thanks in all circumstances? Let's zoom out a bit and look at what is going on in the big picture. What had happened? What was happening? In context, what was Paul saying?

The Thessalonians were concerned that they might not be prepared for the Lord's return. They had experienced persecution and the unexpected death of several fellow believers, which led to some self-evaluation...and worry. In chapter 5, Paul reminded them that there will be no warning before Christ returns. He will come when He's least expected, and those who do not believe will not know what hit them! The believers who have been faithful will be ready for His return because they have already been living in a way that prepares them to meet Him.

So, how were the Thessalonians supposed to live so they were ready? How do we ensure that *we* are ready?

Paul calls faithful Christians *"children of light, children of the day"* and the unbelieving world those *"of the night or of the darkness"*

(1 Thessalonians 5:5). That is a stark comparison, isn't it? But it is a good comparison that helps us to visualize exactly what it looks like to be a believer or a nonbeliever. After this description, Paul gives them instructions for what is considered to be faithful living. The believer should be hardworking and joyful, live peacefully, and pray constantly. To be joyful is evidence of our relationship with Christ because it is a fruit of the Spirit.

Paul was a living example of the things he taught. He wrote to the church at Philippi from prison. Even though he was in chains, he chose to rejoice. His decision to be joyful was more powerful than his trials because it was a work of the Holy Spirit in his life. The joy he experienced came because he trusted in Christ and therefore had an eternal perspective.

SOMETHING TO THINK ABOUT

We can obey and make ourselves ready for the second coming of Christ by directing our focus to all we have in Jesus and by choosing to walk in the Spirit. By yielding to His will and direction in our lives and by walking consistently in the Spirit, His fruit (joy!) will be evident.

Paul's instructions are easier to follow when we consider the verse in context and gain an understanding of what is meant. Praying without ceasing is doable when we realize it simply means we should pray frequently and repeatedly. In fact, it is kind of encouraging to think of prayer as an ongoing conversation with God that shows our trust and dependence on Him. Like a text or phone call to a friend, we can lift up a prayer whenever or wherever we choose.

Giving thanks in everything is evidence that you recognize God's sovereignty and know that He has a purpose for you as well as a plan that is good. It is a language of trust. This is part of what it means to be conformed into the image of Christ. We will grow stronger in all areas of life as we fellowship with God by spending time in His Word and yielding ourselves to Him. He is the One who enables us to be ready for His coming.

EXTRA VERSES FOR STUDY OR PRAYER

Matthew 5:12; Romans 5:3; Philippians 4:4; James 1:2.

VERSES OF THE DAY

Rejoice always, pray without ceasing, give thanks in all circumstances; for this is the will of God in Christ Jesus for you.
—1 Thessalonians 5:16–18

PRAYER

Father, I want to choose to live above my circumstances and find my joy in you. I know that I can only do that by focusing on You and Your promises. Please make me more sensitive to the prompting of the Holy Spirit so that I might hear Your still small voice telling me when my focus is on my circumstances and not on You.

THINK:

PRAY:

PRAISE:

_____

_____

_____

TO DO: PRAYER LIST:

_____   _____

_____   _____

_____   _____

QUESTIONS FOR DEEPER REFLECTION

1. How can a person live above their circumstances spiritually? Why is it important to learn how to do that?

_____

_____

2. What three things does today's verse tell you to do that will help you live above your circumstances so you can find joy?

_____

_____

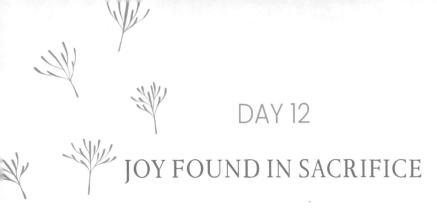

DAY 12

JOY FOUND IN SACRIFICE

READ ROMANS 12

Rejoice in hope, be patient in tribulation, be constant in prayer. —Romans 12:12

My husband grew up putting together puzzles with his family. Even after we were married, whenever we would visit his parents, you would normally see a puzzle in progress atop a small card table in the corner of the living room. There's something about sitting together around a table and looking for just the right piece for an open spot. It's a good time to talk, relax, and feel a sense of accomplishment when you finish your little corner of the puzzle.

As I was reading the chapter and verse for today, the picture of a puzzle came to my mind. The book of Romans contains so many important commands, it's almost as if it were composed of hundreds of puzzle pieces. If Paul's letter to the Romans *were* a puzzle, it would be called *"a living sacrifice"* (verse 1), and the commands would be the puzzle pieces that, when put together, make up a picture of what a life lived as a sacrifice to God looks like.

The book of Romans is a call to believers to present our lives as a living sacrifice. One who answers this calling habitually puts aside his own desires and chooses to prioritize the desires or needs of other people. He does this for the Lord and for those around him. He doesn't do it grudgingly or because he has to do it, but because he is joyfully serving God and sees this as a privilege.

Romans 12 explains that the *"living sacrifice"* life is character-ized by one who seeks wholeheartedly after God and chooses to put his life aside so that he can know and serve God. He puts aside what he has envisioned for his life and yields himself to what God has planned for him. He finds his fulfillment and joy in serving God and others, expecting God to provide for his needs, and all that he does has eternity in mind.

SOMETHING TO THINK ABOUT

How might we live out Romans 12:12?

REJOICE IN HOPE

This does not mean to imply that we will always feel happy. It simply means that we live with eternity in mind. We strive to have God's perspective. Learning and taking on God's perspective gives us hope because we become familiar with what it means to have *"a living hope...an inheritance that is imperishable, undefiled, and unfad-ing, kept in heaven for you"* (1 Peter 1:3–4).

BE PATIENT IN TRIBULATION

Pain and hardship are a part of our daily lives. They are chal-lenges we will have to deal with in the fallen, sinful world we live in. Paul reminds us that our struggles here on earth pale in com-parison to the joy waiting for us in heaven. (See Romans 8:18.) With this in mind, we are called to patiently endure the present suffering with the future in mind.

BE CONSTANT IN PRAYER

While we suffer the trials of the world and rejoice in the hope of what awaits us in eternity, we must choose to pray and connect with the One who can sustain us and give us the strength to per-severe until the end. This will draw us near to the One who has promised that there is more to this life than what we see.

We offer ourselves up as a living sacrifice when we die to our natural, emotion-driven way of responding to the hardships of life.

There is sacrifice in not falling into despair but choosing to rejoice in hope.

There is sacrifice in not giving in to negative emotions but choosing to be patient in tribulation.

There is sacrifice in not letting your mind get lazy but choosing to be constant in prayer.

This is a piece of the *"living sacrifice"* puzzle.

EXTRA VERSES FOR STUDY OR PRAYER

Psalm 16:9–11; Habakkuk 3:18; Romans 5:2; 15:13.

VERSE OF THE DAY

Rejoice in hope, be patient in tribulation, be constant in prayer.   —Romans 12:12

PRAYER

Father, I want to offer up my life as a sacrifice to You. Please enable me to seek You wholeheartedly and choose to put my life aside so that I might know You and serve You better. I offer You any dreams I might have and yield myself to what You have planned for me. Help me to rejoice in hope, be patient in affliction, and constant in prayer. I need You! Amen.

THINK:

_____

_____

_____

PRAY:

_____

_____

_____

PRAISE:

_____

_____

_____

TO DO: PRAYER LIST:

QUESTIONS FOR DEEPER REFLECTION

1. What can you do in order to be _"patient in tribulation"_?

_____

_____

_____

2. Why is joy the result of living a sacrificial life?

_____

_____

_____

DAY 13

JOY FOUND IN COMFORT

READ PSALM 94

When I am filled with cares, Your comfort brings me joy.
—Psalm 94:19 (HCSB)

Have you ever been hurt, betrayed, or slandered by someone within the church—someone who is a brother or sister in Christ? I really believe that this kind of hurt or betrayal is the hardest of all to process because while we don't expect nonbelievers to act in a godly fashion, we do expect it from fellow Christians. When the oppressor is someone who identifies as a brother or sister in Christ, the shock and hurt run deep. When we hope for support, understanding, grace, kindness, and assuming the best, it hurts to experience rejection, judgment, abuse, slander, and sarcasm.

In Psalm 94, God's people were suffering at the hands of those who were considered to be among His own people. They were heaping a weight of evil on this community and getting away with it. Damage had been done and people's lives destroyed. The psalmist stood amidst the destruction and cried out to God. Then he reminded himself of God's promises that were there to cling to when he faced what seemed like impossible circumstances, and he found comfort.

SOMETHING TO THINK ABOUT

Satan wants to do all that he can to destroy and divide God's church. When we go through suffering at the hand of one of

God's own people, there may be a temptation to walk away from the church and from God altogether. Our faith might be shaken. But we can rise above the sinful actions of a brother or sister and focus on the promises of God that our sufferings will train us for righteousness (see Psalm 94:12), He will make us *"more than conquerors"* (Romans 8:37), and He will repay those who have hurt and mistreated us (see Romans 12:19). Clinging to the Word of God will sustain us in these difficult trials brought on by other believers. There is no care too deep that the Word of God, and the promises found there, can't provide comfort and joy for those who seek it.

God is aware of every evil act and will one day bring justice. He's also still working in the lives of those who hurt us. We can rest in this truth and find joy amidst our trial.

EXTRA VERSES FOR STUDY OR PRAYER

Psalm 37:4; Psalm 61:2; Isaiah 57:18; 66:13.

VERSE OF THE DAY

When I am filled with cares, Your comfort brings me joy.
—Psalm 94:19 HCSB

PRAYER

Father, I so easily become anxious and look for ways that I can control what is going on around me. Yet, all I need to do is simply lift my eyes to You and offer You my anxiety. Thank You for the reminder in Psalm 46:10 to *"be still, and know"* that You are God, for Your Word is the only place that I find comfort and refreshment. Your consolation brings me joy in the midst of difficult circumstances.

THINK:

_____

_____

_____

PRAY:

_____

_____

_____

PRAISE:

_____

_____

_____

TO DO: PRAYER LIST:

_____   _____

_____   _____

_____   _____

QUESTIONS FOR DEEPER REFLECTION

1. What circumstances in your life are causing you to be
    "filled with cares"? Prayerfully identify them before the
    Lord, and give them to Him.

_____

_____

_____

2. Have you been hurt by someone whom you considered to be a brother or sister in Christ? How has that affected your relationship with God? Take time to pray that the Holy Spirit will do His work in their life.

3. What do you need to do when you feel anxious and overwhelmed with the cares of this world? How can you experience God's comfort?

DAY 14

JOY FOUND IN GIVING

READ 2 CORINTHIANS 9

Each one must give as he has decided in his heart, not reluc-
tantly or under compulsion, for God loves a cheerful giver.
— 2 Corinthians 9:7

Some of my sweetest memories are of how God has provided for our family over the thirty-three years my husband and I have been married. I was a stay-at-home mom and homeschooled both of our children, which meant that we had to make do on one salary in an area with a high cost of living. We were also in a ministry position that did not pay very much. There were months that we wondered how we would pay all of our bills.

Living this way strengthened our faith; we learned to rely on God for our basic needs. We knew that we had been called to the ministry and our income did not surprise or concern God. Time after time, when it looked like we had a need we couldn't meet, God met that need through one of his generous children. Some days, His provision was money in an envelope that some anonymous donor left in our mailbox. One night, our microwave broke down, and someone left a brand new one on our front porch the next day. There were even some generous people who let us use their beachfront condo when they discovered that we hadn't had a vacation in a long time.

I could tell you story after story of how God has provided for us over the years, and each one brings with it the name of a believer who found great joy in helping to provide for our needs. Seeing people live so generously over the years was used to give me a desire to live in the same way. Now that both of our children are grown and married, and my husband is working a different job, we are more financially able to come to the aid of those who have a need. What joy we find when we are able to serve in the way we have been served so many times in the past!

SOMETHING TO THINK ABOUT

In 2 Corinthians 9, we learn what it means to give willingly and cheerfully. Giving from what God has provided for us should never be done out of obligation or under the weight of legalism. God's desire is that we view giving to meet the needs of others as a privilege. It's a way for God to be glorified when His heart is seen through the actions and generosity of His people. It will provoke those whose needs are met, and those who are able to meet a need, to thankfulness.

Joyfully giving to meet the needs of others is a ministry given to us by God. It is one of the ways we can be the hands and feet of Jesus. After seeing firsthand the many creative ways God has provided for my family over the years, I look forward to being used in that same way in years to come. It is a joyful investment in the lives of others that will count for eternity.

EXTRA VERSES FOR STUDY OR PRAYER

Deuteronomy 15:10; 1 Chronicles 29:9; Proverbs 11:25; Romans 12:8; 2 Corinthians 8:12; Philemon 1:14.

VERSE OF THE DAY

Each one must give as he has decided in his heart, not reluctantly or under compulsion, for God loves a cheerful giver.
—2 Corinthians 9:7

PRAYER

Father, please work within my heart a desire to give freely, generously, and cheerfully, from all that You have given me. None of what I have is mine to hold on to. I offer it to You to use in any way You decide You want to use it, for Your glory.

THINK:

_____

_____

_____

PRAY:

_____

_____

_____

PRAISE:

_____

_____

_____

TO DO: PRAYER LIST:

_____   _____

_____   _____

_____   _____

QUESTIONS FOR DEEPER REFLECTION

1. Can you think of a time when you served someone with a reluctant heart? If so, why did you feel that way?

2. What keeps you from giving to others freely, generously, and cheerfully? What can you do to change?

DAY 15

JOY FOUND IN THE GOD OF MY SALVATION

READ HABAKKUK 3

Though the fig tree should not blossom, nor fruit be on the vines, the produce of the olive fail and the fields yield no food, the flock be cut off from the fold and there be no herd in the stalls, yet I will rejoice in the LORD; I will take joy in the God of my salvation. —Habakkuk 3:17–18

The year 2012 ushered me and my family into a long season of loss and unknowns. Because of some poor decisions made by people in leadership, the ministry we had been a part of for more than twenty-five years shut its doors for good. This left my husband without a job and us without a ministry. Overnight, we were thrust into the unknown, and our lives went from being filled with ministry, people, and purpose, to quiet, questioning, and adrift.

While we were still grieving from the loss of what had been a 24/7 ministry we loved, both of my husband's parents, who were our biggest support system and cheerleaders, passed away within two years of each other. During these life changes, I entered into the mysterious world of anxiety and depression. Disoriented and stunned by life's turn of events—not knowing what the future held, what our purpose was, or what God was doing in our lives—we faced each day relying on God to help us put one foot in front of the other.

It felt like winter had settled in and God had gone silent.

In Habakkuk 3, we see the prophet making a choice amidst some difficult and disturbing circumstances. He was troubled by what he saw going on in the world around him and was living in uncertain times. It seemed to him like God was unable to see what was happening, like He had turned a blind eye to his circumstances. In the beginning of the chapter, we see Habakkuk spend some time in a prayer of lament, suggesting to God what he thought He should do. He ends the chapter with a prayer of trust, acknowledging that God knows best and he will trust God to do what is best even though things look very hopeless.

He learned that he could trust God, and with that trust came great joy, not in his circumstances but in God Himself. He confidently ends this chapter with this prayer:

> Yet I will rejoice in the LORD; I will take joy in the God of my salvation. GOD, the Lord, is my strength; he makes my feet like the deer's; he makes me tread on my high places.
> —Habakkuk 3:18–19

SOMETHING TO THINK ABOUT

Are you in a time of unknowns? Have you been through a season where God seems to have gone silent and you have been forced to live one day at a time, not knowing what the future holds? Can you relate to Habakkuk and how he wanted to tell God how to work in his circumstances? I understand how that feels! Thankfully, as we draw near to God, He enables us to persevere and leads us through these hard seasons.

Like Habakkuk, God has used the season of unknowns and loss that my family and I have gone through to teach us what it means to find joy in our salvation instead of our circumstances. He reminded us that His glory is what is most important. We are broken people who have been given a desire to pour out our lives for God and His purposes. We are gradually sensing His direction.

The curtains have slowly opened and the light has exposed some of what God has been doing in the waiting.

The frigid winter, with its cold, swirling winds, stung our cheeks and blinded us, making it hard to see even two steps in front of us. It brought about much death, as winter always does, making room for something new. We have begun to feel the warm sun on our faces, see the buds of new growth, and smell the fresh spring air. We are amazed at the beauty that was being cultivated in the silence and in the unknown.

I promise you that this will be your experience as well. Just keep clinging!

EXTRA VERSES FOR STUDY OR PRAYER

First Samuel 2:1; Isaiah 61:10; Luke 1:47; Romans 5:2–3; Philippians 4:4.

VERSES OF THE DAY

Though the fig tree should not blossom, nor fruit be on the vines, the produce of the olive fail and the fields yield no food, the flock be cut off from the fold and there be no herd in the stalls, yet I will rejoice in the LORD; I will take joy in the God of my salvation.   —Habakkuk 3:17–18

PRAYER

Father, thank You for Your gift of salvation. I know that no matter what happens, You have given me eternal life. There is nothing that happens to me here in this lifetime that is out of Your control, and no one can snatch me out of Your hand, as Jesus promised in John 10:28. No matter what is going on around me, when I focus on this truth, I find such joy in You!

THINK:

_____

_____

_____

PRAY:

_____

_____

_____

PRAISE:

_____

_____

_____

TO DO: PRAYER LIST:

_____   _____

_____   _____

_____   _____

QUESTIONS FOR DEEPER REFLECTION

1. Is there something in your life keeping you from rejoicing in the Lord and finding joy in the God of your salvation?

_____

_____

_____

2. What can you do in order to fully rejoice and find joy in God?

_____

_____

_____

DAY 16

JOY FOUND IN GOD'S PRESENCE

READ PSALM 16

You make known to me the path of life; in your presence there is fullness of joy; at your right hand are pleasures forevermore. —Psalm 16:11

Let's pretend that you and I are sitting at my kitchen table. We both have a steaming cup of coffee in front of us and we are enjoying the short respite from our busy, daily schedules. Just for fun, and in an attempt to get to know each other better, we start to share with each other what our favorite things are—food, color, place to vacation, hobbies, music, and places to shop. These are the things that come to mind when we think of what makes up who we are and what brings us joy, on a human level. These are things that we consider to be good! We laugh and marvel at how many of these good things we both enjoy that are very similar and, when you leave to go home, we have a sense that we actually know each other a little bit better.

The book of Psalms was written by several authors. Half of them were written by David, but the psalms are not about him or any other author. It is a book about God. If we read through this book and pay attention to all of the good things there, we are able to learn more about God, who He is, what He has done, and what He is like. With each word that tells us more about God, we are able to get a glimpse of a characteristic of Him, and it helps us to know Him better.

In Psalm 16, we see David taking time to proclaim all that God is for him. Taking time to remember helps David solidify why he knows God will take care of him and preserve him. He is receiving strength from what He knows about God...that He is a refuge, a treasure, sovereign, and a counselor. Then he says with confidence that he knows God *will* preserve him, *will* keep him, and *will* guard him.

How was he able to find his confidence in God? By rehearsing in his mind the things he had come to know about Him. And because he knows his God, and has put his trust in Him, David has a confidence that cannot be shaken. This is a God he has come to know and in whom he can place his trust. He has found contentment in God's care, and finds joy in the fact that this life and hope will last for eternity.

SOMETHING TO THINK ABOUT

I love this psalm! Bible commentator Matthew Henry called Psalm 16 "a golden Psalm in the midst of trials." Isn't that a wonderful description? In the same way that you and I might spend a relaxing morning over coffee getting to know a little bit about each other, we can get to know God when we open the book of Psalms and pinpoint any and all of His characteristics and the good things He has done. Just like David, we will be filled with gratefulness, find joy in His presence, and have a confident heart as we remember His faithfulness to us.

EXTRA VERSES FOR STUDY OR PRAYER

Job 36:11; Psalm 11:7; Psalm 17:15; Psalm 21:6; Psalm 43:4.

VERSE OF THE DAY

You make known to me the path of life; in your presence there is fullness of joy; at your right hand are pleasures forevermore.   —Psalm 16:11

PRAYER

Father, thank You for drawing me to Yourself. I know that I would not know You unless You had opened my eyes to my need for You. Thank You for removing the blinders from my eyes and showing me how You want me to live my life. Help me today to live in Your presence, be tuned into Your Spirit, and to seek first Your kingdom and Your righteousness because that is where true joy is found.

THINK:

_____

_____

_____

PRAY:

_____

_____

_____

PRAISE:

_____

_____

_____

TO DO: PRAYER LIST:

_____   _____

_____   _____

_____   _____

QUESTIONS FOR DEEPER REFLECTION

1. Can you think of a time when you sensed God's clear guidance in your life? How did He make it clear to you?

_____

_____

_____

2. Do you need clear guidance right now? How does God make known the path of life?

_____

_____

_____

DAY 17

JOY FOUND IN
OUR PLACE IN CHRIST

READ GALATIANS 5

But the fruit of the Spirit is love, joy, peace, patience, kindness, goodness, faithfulness, gentleness, self-control; against such things there is no law. —Galatians 5:22–23

My daughter-in-law Nicole is one of the sweetest, most compassionate, and loving people I know. She is also a nurse. That's a great combination, isn't it? I have no doubt that God has called her into nursing so that He can use her and her giftings in an extraordinary way!

Recently Nicole shared with me that she not only wants to be a good nurse, but she also yearns to support and encourage other nurses. She has seen some examples of nurses who have been less than helpful, especially to new nurses. Nicole feels called to step in and go against that stereotype. Rather than be one who is in competition with other nurses, she wants to help them succeed. Isn't that amazing?

What would cause Nicole to have that desire? For starters, she has been gifted a personality that is very charitable and warmhearted. She's what the world might call a natural at it. She is gifted in loving others, yes, but she has something else that is motivating her and making her who she is. She is a growing Christian, and the Holy Spirit indwells and empowers her.

Galatians 5 breaks down what it means to have the characteristics that are produced in us by God. These characteristics are evidence that we truly know Him. Paul's letter to the church at Galatia listed what those who are in Christ should see evident in their lives. This is a list of the nine characteristics that make up what he called *"the fruit of the Spirit."* Those who are in Christ and who allow the Holy Spirit to lead them will see these characteristics growing and flowing from their lives. One is not more important than the other; there will be evidence of all of them if we are yielded to the Spirit's work in our lives.

SOMETHING TO THINK ABOUT

If you are *"in Christ"*—something to which Paul referred more than a hundred times in his epistles—you have been set free from the rigid requirements of the Mosaic law, which is a list of rules that few of us could ever keep. Knowing and walking in the freedom that we have as adopted members of God's family is amazing! But it's important to remember that our freedom is not there only to serve ourselves and our desires, since some of the things under the law are now acceptable. It is important to remember that when the fruit of the Spirit takes over who we are, lovingly serving others should be our goal. When we are in Christ, we need to practice allowing God to lead us into Holy Spirit-infused service to others that is motivated by love.

These godly character qualities that are produced by the Holy Spirit are all ones that Jesus lived out in the Gospels. In the same way that my sweet daughter-in-law seeks to live out these qualities as a nurse, our lives can be ones that allow God's love to impact those we come in contact with when we simply yield to the Spirit's leading and allow Him to infiltrate all parts of our lives.

EXTRA VERSES FOR STUDY OR PRAYER

Romans 14:17; 1 Corinthians 13; Ephesians 5:9; 1 Thessalonians 1:6.

VERSES OF THE DAY

But the fruit of the Spirit is love, joy, peace, patience, kindness, goodness, faithfulness, gentleness, self-control; against such things there is no law.   —Galatians 5:22–23

PRAYER

Father, I want Your Holy Spirit to lead and control me, regardless of what may happen today. I pray that the fruit of Your Spirit in my life would flow from my mouth, my actions, my responses, and my attitudes. Help me remember that all is well because I am adopted by You, and that this confidence would be evident in how I live.

THINK:

_____

_____

_____

PRAY:

_____

_____

PRAISE:

_____

_____

_____

TO DO:

_____

_____

_____

PRAYER LIST:

_____

_____

_____

QUESTIONS FOR DEEPER REFLECTION

1. How can you continue to grow in godly character qualities?

_____

_____

2. If you were to ask a friend what fruit(s) of the Spirit they saw in you, what do you think their answer would be?

_____

_____

3. Do you see any areas in your life you would like to grow in?

_____

_____

4. What can you do in order for the fruit of the Spirit to be more evident in your life?

_____

_____

DAY 18

JOY FOUND IN GOD'S WORD

READ PSALM 119:89–112

Your testimonies are my heritage forever, for they are the joy of my heart. —Psalm 119:111

Psalm 119 clearly celebrates the Word of God as being one of His most precious gifts to us. There is no better place to go in order to get to know God and what He desires from His people. In this psalm, it's clear that the author did everything he could to be soaked in God's Word. He read it, listened to it being read aloud, meditated on it, and valued it over any other thing.

The Bible is really the most valuable book that we have at our disposal. Here is a list of what the Bible is for us:

+ It is *"living and active, sharper than any two-edged sword"* (Hebrews 4:12).

+ It is a lamp to our feet and a light to our paths. (See Psalm 119:105.)

+ *"The Word was God"* (John 1:1).

+ *"All Scripture is breathed out by God and profitable for teaching, for reproof, for correction, and for training in righteousness, that the man of God may be complete, equipped for every good work"* (2 Timothy 3:16–17).

+ Christ's words *"will not pass away"* (Matthew 24:35).

+ His Word is *"the truth, and the truth will set you free"* (John 8:32).

✦ *"The word of our God will stand forever"* (Isaiah 40:8).

✦ *"Every word of God proves true"* (Proverbs 30:5).

✦ When stored up in our heart, it helps us to avoid sinning against God. (See Psalm 119:11.)

✦ It *"gives light"* and *"imparts understanding to the simple"* (Psalm 119:130).

SOMETHING TO THINK ABOUT

God's Word introduces us to the God of love and His commandments that were written because He loves us and wants what is best for us. By being in God's Word, getting to know Him, and having our eyes opened to the God of love, we will begin to sense that we are growing in our love toward the One who loved us first. Suddenly we will find that our obedience to Him is becoming motivated by our love for Him. God wants to increase our capacity to have a greater love for Him and for His Word to become the joy of our heart. Isn't that encouraging? All we have to do is pray for Him to daily increase our love for Him.

We see Paul praying such a prayer for himself and the church at Philippi:

> *And it is my prayer that your love may abound more and more, with knowledge and all discernment, so that you may approve what is excellent, and so be pure and blameless for the day of Christ, filled with the fruit of righteousness that comes through Jesus Christ, to the glory and praise of God.*
> —Philippians 1:9–11

We truly can grow in our love for God and His Word, but we must make the effort to soak ourselves in it and get to know the God who loves us. We must ask Him, day by day, to increase our love for Him. And we must not grow weary in seeking Him.

EXTRA VERSES FOR STUDY OR PRAYER

Psalm 119:14, 127, 159–160, 161–162.

VERSE OF THE DAY

Your testimonies are my heritage forever, for they are the joy of my heart. —Psalm 119:111

PRAYER

Father, thank You for Your Word, the Bible. It tells me about Your attributes, about how wise, powerful, and good You are. It shows me how You want me to live, and when I spend time in the truth of Your Word, You somehow use it to renew my mind and Your Spirit changes my heart attitudes. Please cause me to treasure it more than anything this world can offer me. Only You can provide true joy, and You are the only thing in this life that cannot be taken away from me.

THINK:

_____

_____

_____

PRAY:

_____

_____

_____

PRAISE:

_____

_____

_____

TO DO: PRAYER LIST:

_____   _____

_____   _____

_____   _____

QUESTIONS FOR DEEPER REFLECTION

1. What does it mean for God's Word to be the joy of your heart?

_____

_____

2. Is God's Word the joy of your heart? If not, how can you get to that point?

_____

_____

DAY 19

JOY FOUND
IN PROMOTING PEACE

READ PROVERBS 12

Those who promote peace have joy. —Proverbs 12:20 (NIV)

My son Caleb is a very wise man who has a way of looking at life through an objective lens. Although it can take some
time for him to do so, when he finally opens up or shares his
opinions and thoughts about something, you can tell they are
well-formulated. He's been this way for as long as I can remember, and God used him in my life even when he was very young.
His questions and refusal to conform have led me to stop,
think, and pray through things thoroughly and thoughtfully.
Even though there have been times this has frustrated me,
more often than not, many of my views and thoughts have been
altered because he has challenged me to think things through
from a different perspective.

One of the things that I love (most of the time!) when
talking with Caleb is that he will often play devil's advocate in
our conversations. He will argue an opinion or take a side he
doesn't even necessarily agree with in order to force me to think
through issues logically. Taking the time to think in this way
often calms me down and softens my heart toward the other
side as I remember there are usually more ways to view an issue
than just mine.

SOMETHING TO THINK ABOUT

Having someone in our lives who helps us think things through like Caleb does for me can bring our minds and hearts into a calm, peaceful way of responding to people or life when we are facing a challenge. I am so grateful for how God has used my son.

Another vital tool we have at our disposal is God's Word. No matter what we are facing, if we take the time to pray and think in the way we are instructed in the Scriptures, God will use His *"living and active"* Word (Hebrews 4:12) to soften our hearts and help us see how to respond to our circumstances and relationships in a godly way.

In Proverbs 12, we see the contrast Solomon makes between a wise, righteous person and a wicked fool, and the different ways in which they speak. We also learn from the Proverbs that the words coming out of our mouths are a reflection of our heart's condition.

Listening to the objective voice of reason from godly people, soaking in the Word, and allowing God to give you His perspective will help you to respond in a peaceful manner, helping others find peace as well. When we approach our circumstances with a kind heart and help others do the same, we are given the gift of joy, knowing that we have responded in a Christlike way.

EXTRA VERSES FOR STUDY OR PRAYER

Proverbs 1:33; 12:19–21; Matthew 5:9; 1 Peter 3:13.

VERSE OF THE DAY

Those who promote peace have joy.   —Proverbs 12:20 NIV

PRAYER

Father, today may I be one who is a blessing to those around me because I choose to be an instrument of Your peace. I make it my goal, as I interact with the precious people who cross my path, to be a person who helps others focus on You so they might find true peace and joy. Help me to soak in Your Word so that I can be changed and see things from Your perspective.

THINK:

_____

_____

_____

PRAY:

_____

_____

_____

PRAISE:

_____

_____

_____

TO DO:

_____

_____

_____

PRAYER LIST:

_____

_____

_____

QUESTIONS FOR DEEPER REFLECTION

1. Would you consider yourself to be a person who promotes peace? Explain your answer.

_____

_____

_____

2. If you are not one who promotes peace, how is that
   affecting you? How does it affect others? What can you
   do to change?

_____

_____

_____

DAY 20

JOY FOUND IN HOPE

READ PROVERBS 10

The hope of the righteous brings joy, but the expectation of the wicked will perish. —Proverbs 10:28

Are you making your way through this life, with all the suffering that comes with it, facing a hopeless end, seeing only condemnation in your future? Or are you making your way through this life, with all of the suffering that comes with it, knowing there is a purpose in all that you go through and understanding that in eternity, all things will make sense and be made new?

You can face your future with purpose, hope, and joy!

Proverbs 10 contrasts the life of the righteous, who pursue godliness, with the wicked, who chase after sin. We get a glimpse of how these two different kinds of people live and think, how they speak, and the attitudes of their hearts. And we see what their ultimate end will be.

No matter what we are facing today, we can face it with a hope that there is more to this life than what we are going through in the present. We can find joy in our affliction when we are reminded that God is using every single bit of it to make us more like Him and to prepare us for eternity.

In Proverbs 10, we see that the wicked one has no hope, no purpose, and no joy.

SOMETHING TO THINK ABOUT

Something that I once heard from a pastor has stuck with me. He used to say, "The longest a trial can last is a lifetime!" These words instantly put life into perspective for me. The righteous person has hope when he faces trials; he doesn't need to despair because he knows that the longest a trial can last is a lifetime—a fleeting moment compared to eternity. We can have joy in spite of difficulty because we have the hope of heaven. There is no need to despair, even if our trials are lifelong. Our days are in His hands, our security is in Him, and He can use any of our problems to help us grow, if we let Him.

EXTRA VERSES FOR STUDY OR PRAYER

Psalm 16:9; Proverbs 11:23; Habakkuk 3:18; Romans 5:2; 12:12.

VERSE OF THE DAY

The hope of the righteous brings joy, but the expectation of the wicked will perish. —Proverbs 10:28

PRAYER

Father, You say that if I seek You and Your ways, my future will be filled with joy, yet I can so easily be pulled into despair or become overwhelmed when I look at the world around me or focus on my circumstances. Please help me to keep my focus on You and Your promises of what lies ahead. I am Your child.

THINK:

_____

_____

_____

PRAY:

_____

_____

_____

PRAISE:

_____

_____

_____

TO DO: PRAYER LIST:

_____   _____

_____   _____

_____   _____

QUESTIONS FOR DEEPER REFLECTION

1. Do you find yourself feeling overwhelmed when you look around and see all that is going on in our world? When that happens, what do you do?

_____

_____

2. According to Scripture, what can we do when we feel overwhelmed so that we have the correct perspective and experience biblical joy?

_____

_____

DAY 21

JOY FOUND IN GOD'S FAITHFULNESS

For the next ten days, we will be reading and praying passages of Scripture that are examples of a prayer of lament, or an aspect of such a prayer. Please read the entire chapter of the Scripture given each day so that you can see the prayer of lament that we are focusing on.

READ PSALM 40

We had been in a season of change and trial when I woke up and immediately felt completely overwhelmed by our life circumstances. Although I wanted to remain curled up under my warm comforter and forget about everything, I slowly climbed out of bed. I could tell this was going to be one of those days that I was going to have to choose to put one foot in front of the other. I was again entering into the mental battle of having to decide what to do next. As I went about my morning routine, the circumstances that were weighing me down seemed to get heavier and heavier with each passing moment.

Finally, a sense of determination grew within me. I was not going to allow this feeling of being overwhelmed to take over and steal the day. I went to my office, sat down in the soft armchair that sits in the corner of the room, and began to pray. Mentally, I went all the way back to my childhood and began to thank God for the ways in which He had guided, protected, and provided for me over the years. As I thought through each year and each season, God brought to mind the work that He had done in my life and the people He had used to help strengthen me in my walk with Him.

I stayed in that posture of prayer, reflecting on the past, and when I was finished, it was as if a weight had been lifted. Just being reminded of God's faithfulness in my life brought me to a place of peace, and I was able to face the day with confidence that the circumstances we were facing were safe in His hands.

In Psalm 40, we see David doing something similar to what I did that day. (I actually learned it from him!) He is facing a time of desperation and he takes the time to remember. He reflects on how God has delivered him from his enemies in the past. Over and over, he has brought his need for protection to his God; over and over again, God has heard his cry and delivered him.

David then gives thanks to God for the mercies he has experienced over the years. As he gives thanks, he finds the confidence he needs to face the circumstances he is in at present. After David is reminded of God's faithfulness and is given the confidence that he needs to face his circumstances, he then commits to telling others about God's work in his life. David is so grateful and full of joy because of how God has delivered him from his enemies that he praises and worships God and shares this with anyone who will listen. He declares:

> I have told the glad news of deliverance in the great congre-
> gation; behold, I have not restrained my lips, as you know, O
> LORD.   —Psalm 40:9

We also see David crying out to God for His help and inter-vention when he is in need. He remembers God's past faithfulness while asking Him for mercy in yet another thing.

SOMETHING TO THINK ABOUT

I have had to practice this type of prayer of lament more and more as I've gotten older. Life doesn't get easier, and the changes and trials have taught me what it means to be desperate for God. If we can take the time to remember God's faithfulness in our lives, it will give us the hope and faith we need to continue to cry out to Him in our time of need, knowing that He will continue to be faithful. God's grace and mercy are always there, ready to be poured out as we need it today in the same way that it has been in the past.

EXTRA VERSES FOR STUDY OR PRAYER

Genesis 49:1; Psalm 25:3–5; Psalm 27:14.

PRAYER

Father, I feel like there is no stability in my life and there is nothing or no one on whom I can rely. Thank You for how far You have brought me and for all the ways You have provided and been faithful in my life. Please help me to find my stability and joy in You. Help me to persevere so that I can praise You and tell others of Your mighty works, so that others might be encouraged and strengthened by the work You are doing.

THINK:

_____

_____

_____

PRAY:

_____

_____

_____

PRAISE:

_____

_____

_____

TO DO: PRAYER LIST:

_____   _____

_____   _____

_____   _____

QUESTIONS FOR DEEPER REFLECTION

1. Do you sometimes feel like you just can't persevere in your daily callings even one more minute? What do you do when you are faced with that feeling?

_____

_____

_____

2. Take some time to pray and ask God to give you the strength you need to persevere in this difficult time. The enemy of our souls is working overtime to discourage you and get you to quit. Interrupt his efforts by crying out to the Lord for His strength!

_____

_____

_____

3. Write your prayer below.

_____

_____

_____

DAY 22

JOY FOUND IN
THE SEARCH FOR GOD

READ PSALM 34

Fearful. This was not a word that I would have used to describe myself...until I had children. After Brianna and Caleb were born, I became overwhelmed with fear. I was fearful that something might happen to them or that someone might hurt them in some way. I was fearful that they might be exposed to a bad influence. I was fearful that I was a terrible mom, that I would drive them away, or that I would do something wrong and mess them up for good. Fear motivated much of what I did.

Finally, through a series of circumstances, God began to show me that I needed to learn to focus on Him, His character, and His faithfulness, not on all the things that could potentially go wrong. Slowly, ever so slowly, it has become more of a habit to choose to focus on God and not on the potential dangers, but I must be honest with you, it is still a battle.

I love Psalm 34 and the example that David gives us to follow. He seeks the Lord. He seeks Him and he doesn't stop! I think this is an important aspect of the prayer of lament. Seeking God, over and over and over. Not giving up. Continuing to seek Him time and time again. If we don't do this, how will we show Him that we trust Him? How will we remember that He has been faithful if we don't go to Him again and again, allowing Him to remind us?

David sought the Lord and the Lord answered him. He faced anxiety and fear because of the threat he was facing, but what did He do? He prayed! He took time to remember his experiences in the past and they were what God used to strengthen his faith and remind him of who was in control. It's what allowed him to remember that he had no reason to be afraid.

David was also determined to proclaim God's faithfulness and invite others to join him in this praise and worship. We see this in verses 1–3:

> *I will bless the LORD at all times; his praise shall continually be in my mouth. My soul makes its boast in the LORD; let the humble hear and be glad. Oh, magnify the LORD with me, and let us exalt his name together!*

SOMETHING TO THINK ABOUT

If we desire for our fear to be replaced with faith, we must learn to choose, one day at a time, to come before the Lord, express our concerns and feelings, and allow Him to take us down memory lane to the places in our lives where His work and faithfulness have been evident. This process has encouraged me and given me the strength to move forward into the unknown many times, with the confidence I need to trust in the One who has kept me up until this day. It will do the same for you!

EXTRA VERSES FOR STUDY OR PRAYER

Psalm 35:27; Psalm 69:32; Psalm 119:74; Jeremiah 9:24.

PRAYER

Father, I am afraid. There is no one who can deliver me out of this pit of despair but You. I know that my hope is found in You alone. Help me focus on You and not my circumstances and disappointments. Please give me a heart that wants to rejoice in You.

THINK:

_____

_____

_____

PRAY:

_____

_____

_____

PRAISE:

_____

_____

_____

TO DO: PRAYER LIST:

_____   _____

_____   _____

_____   _____

QUESTIONS FOR DEEPER REFLECTION

1. Do you sometimes feel like you are alone and left to fend for yourself? Have even your loved ones disappointed you and let you down?

_____

_____

_____

2. According to the Scriptures, who is the only One who won't let you down, abandon you, or disappoint you? Who is the only One who can deliver you from all your fears?

_____

_____

_____

3. Write your prayer below.

_____

_____

_____

DAY 23

JOY FOUND IN SHARED PAIN

READ PSALM 139

I'll never forget the morning I received *that* phone call from my daughter Brianna.

"Mom, I had a miscarriage last night…"

As my brain tried to catch up to the words my daughter spoke, my mother's heart scrambled to find the words that would comfort so I could make it all better. My precious daughter had just experienced a great loss and there was nothing I could say to fix it. In fact, I hadn't even been able to be there to help her through this painful experience. I didn't even know it had happened until the next morning.

In the weeks following, I spent time with my daughter as she processed the loss that she and her husband had experienced. There were times when she would talk about it and was, understandably, in tears, and there were times when she didn't want to talk about it at all. The trauma of this loss hovered over Brianna and her husband for a while. The idea of starting a family and all that would mean was something they had grown used to and excited about. The precious little one had only been in her womb for a short time, but had already begun to capture their hearts. It took some time to readjust their way of thinking.

Even in their pain, questioning, and heartache, the one thing that held them together was their faith in God. It did not take away the suffering, but it caused them to draw closer to Him with their questions and need for strength and comfort. Among the verses that God brought to my daughter's mind during this difficult time were these:

> You hem me in, behind and before, and lay your hand upon me. Such knowledge is too wonderful for me; it is high; I cannot attain it.   —Psalm 139:5–6

In these verses, David is stating his unwavering confidence in God and the knowledge that He protects and guards His people. God hems them in. In this context, it means the same as guarding a valuable object. God guards His beloved children on all sides and He lays His gentle, reassuring hand upon them no matter where they are or what they are going through.

Every day, even in our hardest sufferings and weakest moments, God is with us and is strengthening us. He is always present and sees it all—every tear, every heartbreak, every threat, and all of our suffering. He sees it and He does not grow weary. Psalm 139 also reminds us that God knows His people and there is no place that we can go that He does not know where we are and what is going on in our lives

SOMETHING TO THINK ABOUT

As her mom, I would love to be there to help Brianna through every single hard time she might face, but I cannot do that. Thankfully, she has a heavenly Father who is there. He knows all there is to know about her. He is the One who will bring verses to her mind when she is hurting to guide her as she faces life's hardships. He is the One who will grow her faith and help her process her circumstances. And He is the One who hems her in, laying His gentle reassuring hand on her like no one else can. He is our ever-present support system.

EXTRA VERSES FOR STUDY OR PRAYER

Psalm 5:8; Psalm 7:9; Psalm 16:11; Psalm 19:1.

PRAYER

Father, sometimes I wish I could actually see You! Please enable me to pick up Your Word and remember all Your promises. Thank You for knowing me, for seeing all that I do and everywhere I go, and for being my ever-present support system. I need You, and I need to sense that You are right beside me.

THINK:

_____

_____

_____

PRAY:

_____

_____

_____

PRAISE:

_____

_____

_____

TO DO: PRAYER LIST:

QUESTIONS FOR DEEPER REFLECTION

1. What do you do when you feel like you are alone? Who do you think is whispering in your ear that you are alone?

_____

_____

_____

2. Take some time to find Scripture verses that tell you who is always with you. Be encouraged by what you find!

_____

_____

_____

DAY 24

JOY FOUND IN GOD'S PROMISES

READ PSALM 102

The title of Psalm 102 in *The Holy Bible, English Standard Version* is "Do Not Hide Your Face from Me. A Prayer of one afflicted, when he is faint and pours out his complaint before the LORD." That is a pretty good description of what this author was feeling, isn't it? This is a prayer of lament from someone in need crying out to God.

Facing unexplained troubles, the psalmist boldly comes before his God and admits he is desperate for Him. He pleads with God, asking Him to not hide His face, but answer him speedily. He spends time lamenting the hardships he has had to endure. It sounds like he is at the end of his rope. He has seen heartbreak, enemies have attacked, and he is acknowledging the reality that life is short. Then there is a shift in focus:

> *But you, O LORD, are enthroned forever; you are remembered throughout all generations....Nations will fear the name of the LORD, and all the kings of the earth will fear your glory.*
> —Psalm 102:12, 15

The psalmist has turned his focus to His God and away from his circumstances. Up until now, we have very clearly seen his pain, but with this shift, he emphatically declares that his hope comes from God's promises. He clings to God and His promises; he knows the Lord will be faithful to His people.

SOMETHING TO THINK ABOUT

As you read through Psalm 102, notice that the psalmist repeatedly acknowledges his own weakness. He then points out the obvious: God is strong and everlasting. He is the One he can count on; He is the One who is faithful and true. He is the only place where hope is found. The writer might have started out feeling hopeless, but he winds up with the reminder that God is still on the throne and that He will give him the strength he needs to persevere to the end. He may not know what the outcome of his difficult circumstances will be, but he trusts the One who does know and who is in control.

All suffering comes to an end, either in this lifetime or the next. Like the psalmist, we have the privilege of knowing that we can trust God and have full confidence in Him, no matter how long it takes for our suffering to end.

We can turn our focus to our God and away from our circumstances, and with this shift, we will see that our hope comes from God's promises. We can find true joy in the midst of difficulty when we cling to God and the knowledge that He will be faithful to His people.

EXTRA VERSES FOR STUDY OR PRAYER

Psalm 39:12; Psalm 61:1; Psalm 119:169; Psalm 142:2.

PRAYER

Father, I am so weary. I need to see You working, to feel Your presence, and to know that You hear me. Please refresh me and bring some encouragement my way. I know that You have been faithful in the past and that You promise to be faithful in the days ahead. You are faithful, and You will be glorified!

THINK:

_____

_____

_____

PRAY:

_____

_____

_____

PRAISE:

_____

_____

_____

TO DO: PRAYER LIST:

_____   _____

_____   _____

_____   _____

QUESTIONS FOR DEEPER REFLECTION

1. Have you ever prayed and asked God to do something
    that will bring refreshment to your soul? Why do you
    think God wants us to ask Him for this?

_____

_____

_____

2. God has been faithful in the past and He will be faithful in the days ahead. What is the ultimate reason He chooses to be faithful?

DAY 25

JOY FOUND IN POURING OUT YOUR HEART

READ PSALM 73

Have you ever gone through what might be called a crisis of faith? A time when life was too hard or didn't make sense, and you wondered if it was even worth it anymore to hold onto a faith that did not seem to be working in your current circumstances? If so, you will find comfort in Psalm 73.

The author, Asaph, begins the psalm by talking about what he sees as he looks around. Those who are not following after God are prospering and he is not. All he can see is that those who are godless and even mock God are thriving. He complains to God and has become bitter. God had promised to take care of him but it didn't really seem as though He was keeping His promise. Asaph was even tempted to join the world and walk away from his faith instead of trusting God.

The prayer of lament gives us permission to come before God and pour out our heart. I love that! We might as well tell Him what we are feeling because He is aware of it anyway! When we tell Him what we are feeling, we enter into a conversation with Him. That gives Him an opportunity to guide our thoughts and remind us of truth. This is exactly what happens in this psalm.

After the psalmist spends time complaining, he enters into a place of worship and the truth shines into the dark and doubting

places of his soul. God is *still* good. His gaze shifts from the world
to His Father and he is lifted above his circumstances to focus on
what will last for eternity.

SOMETHING TO THINK ABOUT

The following truths, all found in Psalm 73:23–28, motivate
us to not walk away from our faith, regardless of what happens
around us:

+ God holds my right hand.

+ God guides me with His counsel.

+ God *"will receive me to glory."*

+ *"God is the strength of my heart."*

+ God is *"my portion forever."*

+ *"It is good to be near God."*

+ God is my refuge.

We can rest and find contentment because we are near God
and have Him as the strength of our heart and portion forever,
regardless of what is going on around us. My greatest need is to
stay near God. When we take time to pray a prayer of lament, we
will always come back to this truth. Being close to God is the best
place to be. Nothing compares to being near God, holding His
hand, heeding His counsel, receiving His strength, and finding
our refuge in Him.

EXTRA VERSES FOR STUDY OR PRAYER

Psalm 17:5; Psalm 38:16; Psalm 94:18; Psalm 116:8.

PRAYER

Father, sometimes it feels like I try in vain to live the way I
am supposed to live. I often feel like I am not having victory or

growing at all. But then I am reminded that You are the One who holds me up, strengthens me every moment, and never leaves me. You are the One I can go to for help and safety. I need You!

THINK:

PRAY:

PRAISE:

TO DO: PRAYER LIST:

---   ---

---   ---

---   ---

QUESTIONS FOR DEEPER REFLECTION

1. Have you ever thought, *Why do I even bother trying?* Where do you think that question comes from? Who do you think wants you to stop persevering?

2. The enemy will do all that he can to get you to give up. To defeat him, we need to interrupt the lies he whispers to us by calling out to the Lord in prayer and in worship. Why don't you do that right now!

DAY 26

JOY FOUND IN SPEAKING
WORDS OF TRUST

READ PSALM 56

For thirty-three years, I have been married to a man who has been a living example to me of what it means to strive to respond biblically in difficult (and all!) circumstances. God has used Brian in countless ways in my life, but there is one in particular that tops the list. He is slow to speak, purposefully pausing to think before he responds. On most nights, as we are turning off the light to go to sleep, I will hear him sigh and then whisper the word, "Father…" That's how I know he is going to begin praying over the things that are weighing heavily on his heart.

Since we have been married for over three decades, we have had ample opportunity to experience God's faithfulness together. Night after night, my sweet husband has reverently lifted our burdens up to God, and time and time again, God has heard his sighs and his prayers. We have quickly become one of those *older* couples who love to talk about our past experiences and how God has worked in our lives. We try not to bore younger people with our stories, but I will be honest with you, it's very difficult to keep them to ourselves!

In today's psalm, we see David going before God again in the same way he has so many times in the past. He describes his circumstances but immediately chooses to respond with a heart that trusts in the God who has shown Himself to be faithful. David explains what is happening to him and then he speaks words of trust. He does this countless times in the Psalms, leaving a pattern of going to God with his burdens and choosing to trust the God of his salvation.

I love his prayer toward the end of this psalm:

> *You have kept count of my tossings; put my tears in your bottle. Are they not in your book? Then my enemies will turn back in the day when I call. This I know, that God is for me. In God, whose word I praise, in the LORD, whose word I praise, in God I trust; I shall not be afraid. What can man do to me?*
> —Psalm 56:8–11

SOMETHING TO THINK ABOUT

After thirty-three years of marriage, I feel like the sighs and the prayers that have been spoken by my husband and me could fill a book. But regardless of how old you are, you can find comfort in the fact that God keeps count of your tossings, puts your tears in a bottle, and keeps track of all of your prayers. He will never grow tired of hearing from you and He wants you to pour your heart out to Him. Doing this is the answer to finding joy and hope amidst the chaos and crisis of life.

You can be assured that God is for you. You can trust Him.

EXTRA VERSES FOR STUDY OR PRAYER

Psalm 35:1; Psalm 55:18; Psalm 57:3; Psalm 119:58.

PRAYER

Father, thank You for caring for every single one of my concerns, whether they are big or small. Thank You for allowing me to come to You with what is burdening me, and thank You for being there for me! I trust You!

THINK:

_____

_____

_____

PRAY:

_____

_____

_____

PRAISE:

_____

_____

_____

TO DO: PRAYER LIST:

_____   _____

_____   _____

_____   _____

QUESTIONS FOR DEEPER REFLECTION

1.   Do you see the value and help of being able to go to God with your concerns and burdens?

_____

_____

_____

2. Does complaining to God seem like something you shouldn't do?

_____

_____

_____

3. What makes it okay to complain or tell God your fears and hurts?

_____

_____

_____

DAY 27

JOY FOUND IN
PRAYING PAST BETRAYAL

READ PSALM 55

Betrayal is the theme of this psalm. You can probably relate to what it feels like to be double-crossed. I don't think many of us make it through this life without experiencing duplicity in some way. And when that betrayal comes from someone who you have considered to be a dear friend, someone with whom you have spent time sharing your deepest thoughts and feelings, it can be devastating.

I've had this happen only a couple of times in my life, and although I eventually accepted it and came to a place where I can see that God has used it for good, I don't think I will ever completely get over the rejection and betrayal. Close friends are hard to come by. It's a rare experience to meet someone with whom you feel so comfortable that you trust them with your heart. For them to turn their back on you sends shock waves that echo for years to come and often makes you hesitant to trust anyone else as much as you did your betrayer.

In Psalm 55, we see that David had been betrayed by a close friend and a familiar companion. It's believed that David here was referring to his own son Absalom as well as his trusted counselor Ahithophel. (See 2 Samuel 15–18.) David is devastated and wants to take refuge in the wilderness. Apparently, his betrayal included some kind of evil, which would be even more painful than mere rejection.

So, what does David do? In verse 22, he says:

Cast your burden on the LORD, *and he will sustain you; he will never permit the righteous to be moved.*

In this statement, he expresses where his strength and comfort come from in this painful circumstance. He is trusting God and His timing in dealing with those who have turned their backs on him.

SOMETHING TO THINK ABOUT

If you have gone through the heartbreaking experience of being rejected and betrayed by someone who had once been a close friend, I want to tell you how very sorry I am that you have gone through that. I understand your pain. I really do. Let me assure you that even if your situation is never resolved, as mine has never been, as the years go by and you get some distance from the experience, God does give you His perspective if you are willing to trust Him with the pain and the circumstances.

You can follow David's godly example found in today's prayer of lament. He brings his complaint, and a detailed description of his pain, to God with the confidence that God hears and sees him. He tells God how badly he is hurting and then he comes to a point of accepting what has happened. He offers the pain, the loss, the rejection, and the betrayal to God, and expresses a desire to see his friend's repentance and restoration. Finally, David trusts God and His timing in how He will deal with the person who has hurt him. His final words in this psalm are, *"But I will trust in you"* (verse 23).

You can trust in Him too.

EXTRA VERSES FOR STUDY OR PRAYER

Psalm 10:1; Psalm 27:9; Psalm 54:2; Psalm 61:1.

PRAYER

Father, I know You understand how it feels to be betrayed, for Your own Son was betrayed and it cost Him His life. Yet, His betrayal was used to fulfill Your great purpose to redeem all of mankind. I trust You to use my experience of betrayal for Your bigger purposes. Help me to trust You to have the final word.

THINK:

_____

_____

_____

PRAY:

_____

_____

PRAISE:

_____

_____

TO DO: PRAYER LIST:

_____   _____

_____   _____

_____   _____

QUESTIONS FOR DEEPER REFLECTION

1. Have you been betrayed by someone who was a dear friend?

2. Does this prayer of lament help you to process your loss?

3. What part of this prayer is hardest for you to pray?

DAY 28

JOY FOUND
IN SEEKING FORGIVENESS

READ PSALM 51

My daughter has always been very sensitive. As soon as she could talk, Brianna began to ask for forgiveness for everything! At night, she couldn't rest unless she had asked for forgiveness for all she had done wrong that day. I can still picture her in her big-girl bed, at the age of three, asking me to forgive her every night before she went to sleep. Even at that very young age, she needed to have a clear conscience so that she could sleep peacefully.

As much as I loved that my little girl had a sensitive heart, I doubted that she had a true sense of the heaviness of sin. We grow in our understanding of our sinfulness as we continue on our journey with God. He softens our heart to be more in tune with the Holy Spirit, which develops our sensitivity to the things that are an offense to Him.

Psalm 51 was written by David after the prophet Nathan confronted him about his sin with Bathsheba and the murder of her husband. God used that confrontation to open David's eyes to the evil he had done, thus causing him to confess and grieve over his sin. This psalm is a good model to follow when we find ourselves in a place of needing forgiveness in the same way David did.

Here, we see David acknowledging his guilt by using three words to describe his offenses:

+ Iniquity: immoral or grossly unjust behavior

+ Transgression: an act that goes against a law, rule, or code of conduct; an offense

+ Sin: an immoral act considered to be a transgression against divine law

By using these three descriptive words, we can see that David knows the depth of his sin against God and His ways. He then finds comfort in the fact that the Holy Spirit dwells within him. This is evident by the fact that He has convicted David of his sin.

We then see David asking for forgiveness, holding on to what he knows about who God is. The Lord is a merciful God who has made a covenant with David, and that is enough. Finally, David experiences joy because he knows he is forgiven and God will keep His promises.

O Lord, open my lips, and my mouth will declare your praise. For you will not delight in sacrifice, or I would give it; you will not be pleased with a burnt offering. The sacrifices of God are a broken spirit; a broken and contrite heart, O God, you will not despise. —Verses 15–17

SOMETHING TO THINK ABOUT

This particular prayer of lament is one prayed by a man who is genuinely grieving over his sin and crying out to God for mercy. After acknowledging all that he has done that is an offense to God, he takes the time to praise and thank God for the undeserved mercy He has poured out on him. May we grow in our understanding of how our sin affects us and offends God, and rejoice in the undeserved grace we have been shown. May we be so very grateful that we do not have to live under the weight of condemnation. And may our confession be more than wanting to rid ourselves of a guilty conscience, but motivated instead by the desire to be in a right relationship with God.

EXTRA VERSES FOR STUDY OR PRAYER

Psalm 22:24; Psalm 34:18; Psalm 147:3; Isaiah 57:15.

PRAYER

Father, I feel so weighed down by my own sinfulness and failure to honor You. Sometimes this is all I can see, and I find myself living under a cloud of condemnation. This is not what You want for me! Thank You that Your Son's death on the cross has covered all of my sin. As I confess my sin, I know that You are faithful to forgive and cleanse me from all unrighteousness. Thank You for restoring me the joy of Your salvation!

THINK:

_____

_____

_____

PRAY:

_____

_____

_____

PRAISE:

_____

_____

_____

TO DO:

_____

_____

_____

PRAYER LIST:

_____

_____

_____

QUESTIONS FOR DEEPER REFLECTION

1. It's easy to focus on our sinfulness and fall into condemnation, isn't it? Who do you think wants us to live under the weight of condemnation? (Hint: it's not God.)

_____

_____

_____

2. Take some time to sit quietly before God and ask Him to bring to mind any unconfessed sin in your life. As He brings it to mind, confess it and accept His unconditional love and forgiveness.

_____

_____

_____

DAY 29

JOY FOUND IN
THE PRAYER OF LAMENT

READ PSALM 46

The prayer of lament is a powerful prayer that helps you process the difficulties of life. Whether you are praying over the sadness in the world or in your own life, this is a prayer that you can pray when you are overwhelmed with what you see going on around you.

I love that it's fine with God for us to come to Him and complain about what we are facing. Who better to go to than the One who is in control of all things, who gives everything in our life meaning, and who will give us a perspective that is not found anywhere else?

The pivotal moment in the prayer of lament is the moment when your focus is redirected and you begin to rest in God as you are reminded of who He is. This is the moment when you begin to rehearse the truths that you know about God.

Let's take a look at a few of the key verses in Psalm 46 and what they say about God. I think it is helpful to read them in a few different translations.

In Psalm 46:1, we see that God is mighty and always ready to help us:

+ *God is our refuge and strength, a very present help in trouble.* (ESV)
+ *God is our refuge and strength [mighty and impenetrable], a very present and well-proved help in trouble.* (AMP)

+ *God is our refuge and strength, a great help in times of distress.* (ISV)

In verse 5, we see that God is with us and will help us at daybreak:

+ *God is within her, she will not fall; God will help her at break of day.* (NIV)

+ *God is in the midst of her; she shall not be moved; God will help her when morning dawns.* (ESV)

+ *Since God is in her midst, she will not be shaken. God will help her at the break of dawn.* (ISV)

In verse 7, we see that the Lord is in charge of the heavenly host and He is our refuge:

+ *The LORD Almighty is with us; the God of Jacob is our fortress.* (NIV)

+ *The LORD of hosts is with us; the God of Jacob is our fortress.* (ESV)

+ *The LORD of armies is with us; the God of Jacob is our stronghold.* (NASB)

+ *The LORD of hosts is with us; the God of Jacob is our stronghold [our refuge, our high tower].* (AMP)

Psalm 46:10 tells us to be still and know that He is God, worthy of all praise and glory:

+ *Be still, and know that I am God; I will be exalted among the nations, I will be exalted in the earth.* (NIV)

+ *Stop striving and know that I am God; I will be exalted among the nations, I will be exalted on the earth.* (NASB)

+ *Be still and know (recognize, understand) that I am God. I will be exalted among the nations! I will be exalted in the earth.* (AMP)

+ *Stop your fighting—and know that I am God, exalted among the nations, exalted on the earth.* (HCSB)

Verse 11, the last verse, drives home the promises of verse 7:

+ *The LORD of hosts is with us; the God of Jacob is our fortress.* (ESV)

+ *The* LORD *of armies is with us; the God of Jacob is our stronghold.* (NASB)

+ *The* LORD *of the heavenly armies is with us; the God of Jacob is our refuge.* (ISV)

SOMETHING TO THINK ABOUT

Many translations of the Psalms, including this one, have the word *"Selah"* at the end of a verse. This is a transliteration of a Hebrew word that is believed to mean "pause." As you pause and begin to focus on God's presence and power rather than on issues that are overwhelming you, you realize that He is your stronghold and much bigger than your circumstances. Focusing on the truths of who God is, and His presence and power in your life, helps you realize that what matters most is the truth about God: He is there and He is stable even when everything else is not.

Selah! Pause and think of that!

EXTRA VERSES FOR STUDY OR PRAYER

Psalm 9:9; Psalm 14:6; Psalm 31:4; Psalm 32:6.

PRAYER

Father, it seems like the world is getting worse by the day. Division, fighting, sickness, and natural disasters—it's overwhelming! Your Word reminds me that You are my strength and where I find refuge. You are the only source of true and lasting help, hope, and peace. It is not found anywhere else. Thank You for providing all that we need to find peace in this life.

THINK:

PRAY:

_____

_____

_____

PRAISE:

_____

_____

_____

TO DO: PRAYER LIST:

_____   _____

_____   _____

_____   _____

QUESTIONS FOR DEEPER REFLECTION

1. Does it seem like the world is falling apart? Do you find it hard to believe some of the things that you have lived through in your lifetime?

_____

_____

2. What does the Word say about who is ultimately in control? Does that give you some comfort?

_____

_____

DAY 30

JOY FOUND IN PRAISING GOD

READ PSALM 28

Blessed be the LORD! For he has heard the voice of my pleas for mercy. The LORD is my strength and my shield; in him my heart trusts, and I am helped; my heart exults, and with my song I give thanks to him. The LORD is the strength of his people; he is the saving refuge of his anointed. Oh, save your people and bless your heritage! Be their shepherd and carry them forever. —Psalm 28:6–9

Let's end this thirty-day journey of praying through the Scriptures, and learning more about biblical joy and the prayer of lament, by focusing on what this psalm tells us about God's character and what that means for us during times of hardship.

The last four verses of Psalm 28 are words we can pray with confidence that our God hears our cry and we realize that we can count on Him. The psalmist, David, has known God's character and His faithfulness in the past, and he is believing in what he knows about God—that He will be faithful again. He is praising God for hearing and answering his prayer.

We see God's trustworthy character when we meditate on verse 7:

The LORD is my strength [might, power] *and my shield* [protection]; *in him my heart* [mind] *trusts, and I am helped;*

my heart exults [is filled with joy], *and with my song I give thanks to him.*

In the last verses, we are reminded of our Savior, Jesus Christ:

The LORD *is the strength of his people* [those who trust in Him]; *he is the saving refuge of his anointed* [Jesus]. *Oh, save your people and bless your heritage! Be their shepherd and carry them forever.*

SOMETHING TO THINK ABOUT

As you read through this psalm, take the time to note what it is telling you about who God is, what God does, what He expects from His people, and how we should respond to Him. In each aspect of God's character, we see Him protecting and preserving His people, not just from physical harm, but also from the punishment we deserve for our sin.

No matter what your future holds, or what you are facing in the moment, when you take the time to focus on the truth of who God is, you will be filled with the hope, confidence, strength, and assurance that God will give you what you need to face each day. You will also know that there is so much more to life than what you see. God is trustworthy; He is here for you now, He will be there for you in the future, and He longs to spend eternity with you.

This is what will bring you joy for today and hope for tomorrow!

EXTRA VERSES FOR STUDY OR PRAYER

Psalm 18:2; Psalm 28:2; Psalm 31:21–22; Psalm 66:19–20.

PRAYER

Father, I pray for the precious person holding this book who has gone through this thirty-day journey with me. I thank You for leading them through this devotional journal and giving them the desire to seek the joy that is found only in You. I pray that they will grow in their understanding of who You are and that they will continually turn to You and be reminded of how You have been faithful in the past and that You will continue to be faithful in the future.

VERSES OF THE DAY

Blessed be the LORD! For he has heard the voice of my pleas for mercy. The LORD is my strength and my shield; in him my heart trusts, and I am helped; my heart exults, and with my song I give thanks to him. The LORD is the strength of his people; he is the saving refuge of his anointed. Oh, save your people and bless your heritage! Be their shepherd and carry them forever. —Psalm 28:6–9

THINK:

PRAY:

PRAISE:

TO DO:

_____

_____

_____

PRAYER LIST:

_____

_____

_____

QUESTIONS FOR DEEPER REFLECTION

1. Think of a time when you faced a circumstance that caused you to be afraid or overwhelmed. What was the circumstance?

_____

_____

_____

2. Can you see how God was faithful to you then? How was He faithful?

_____

_____

_____

3. Does the prayer of lament help you to process hard circumstances and give you hope?

_____

_____

_____

4. How do the prayer of lament and biblical joy fit together?

_____

_____

_____

ABOUT THE AUTHOR

Gina L. Smith is an author, podcaster, and a prayer mentor for Million Praying Moms.

Gina and her husband Brian have been married for more than three decades. They served as the on-campus parents at a Christian college for more than twenty years while Brian was a professor and dean of students. They mentored hundreds of college and seminary students as well as young couples over the years.

Gina has a degree in Bible studies from Washington Bible College/Capital Bible Seminary.

She has written for several organizations, including Million Praying Moms. She is also the author of *Grace Gifts: Practical Ways to Help Your Children Understand God's Grace*.

Gina and Brian have two grown children and reside in the metro area of Washington, D.C.

To connect with Gina, visit www.ginalsmith.com.